# THE DAILY SHADOW

## EMBRACING YOUR INNER VILLAIN

### 366 REFLECTIONS ON HARNESSING YOUR DARK SIDE

JOHN KIMBERLY

Copyright © 2024 John Kimberly

All rights reserved. No part of this book may be reproduced, distributed, or transmitted in any form or by any means, including photocopying, recording, or other electronic or mechanical methods, without the prior written permission of the publisher, except in the case of brief quotations embodied in critical reviews and certain other noncommercial uses permitted by copyright law.

Disclaimer:

This book is intended for personal growth and self-discovery purposes only. It does not advocate or encourage malice, unethical behavior, or any actions that are against the law. The concepts and strategies discussed within are meant to help readers understand and harness their inner strengths responsibly and ethically. Always exercise good judgment and integrity in all your endeavors.

ISBN: 9798333636379

For more information, contact thedailyshadow@hotmail.com

*"It is better to be feared than loved,*
*if you cannot be both."*

- Niccolo Machiavelli

# CONTENTS

# INTRODUCTION

Have you ever wondered why villains in stories captivate us so much? They possess a certain allure, an audacious confidence, and an unyielding determination that often leaves us in awe. What if you could harness those same qualities for your own life? This book is designed to help you unlock the power of your hidden self by understanding and channeling your darker impulses to navigate life's challenges with more control and influence.

Consider historical figures like Genghis Khan, Vlad the Impaler, and Rasputin. Each of them has been cast as a villain in the annals of history, yet they share common traits that contributed to their undeniable influence. Genghis Khan's strategic brilliance enabled him to create one of the largest empires in history. Vlad the Impaler's fierce determination secured his legacy as a defender of his homeland, albeit through brutal methods. Rasputin's enigmatic presence and persuasive power allowed him to navigate the treacherous waters of the Russian court. What do they have in common? An ability to wield their darker qualities with precision and purpose.

Every day, we're faced with situations that require more than just a straightforward approach. Sometimes, a touch of cunning, a dash of resilience, or a bit of strategic thinking can make all the difference. This book offers 366 pieces of daily wisdom to help you tap into these traits. This isn't about embracing evil; it's about using the full spectrum of your personality to achieve your goals.

Society often tells us to suppress our darker sides, viewing them as harmful. But what if these aspects, when managed correctly, could be our greatest assets? This book encourages you to acknowledge these impulses and transform them into sources of strength and influence. By doing so, you can achieve a balanced, powerful, and more authentic version of yourself.

Each entry provides practical advice and reflections on various aspects of villainous wisdom. From mastering subtle manipulation to using secrets strategically, these insights will help you navigate life's complexities more effectively, turning perceived flaws into formidable tools for success.

Imagine possessing the sharpness of a strategist, the determination of a conqueror, and the foresight of a master planner. This book will guide you in cultivating these qualities by embracing your inner villain and using it to enhance your life. You don't have to be malicious to be powerful; you just need to harness your inner strength and shadowy instincts.

This book is your companion on a journey of self-discovery and empowerment, inviting you to explore your character and emerge stronger, wiser, and more influential. Prepare to embark on a transformative journey, navigating the shadows with grace and precision.

Let's begin the journey of embracing your inner villain and unlocking your true potential!

# PART I

# GENESIS

# January

## JANUARY 1ST

# THE POWER OF FEAR

*"The best way to control people is to sow fear into their hearts."*

Fear is a powerful motivator. It can drive people to action, influence their decisions, and shape their behaviors in profound ways. By understanding how fear works, one can manipulate situations to their advantage, ensuring that they remain in control.

Embracing the concept of fear means acknowledging its role in everyday life. From personal relationships to professional endeavors, fear can be used to maintain power dynamics. Learning to instill fear subtly and effectively can transform one's influence over others.

However, wielding fear responsibly is crucial. The goal is not to cause harm or unnecessary suffering but to create a sense of urgency and compliance. Mastering the art of fear can lead to greater success and control in various aspects of life.

## JANUARY 2ND

# THE ALLURE OF CHAOS

*"Chaos is a ladder; those who climb it become kings."*

Chaos often presents opportunities that order does not. In the midst of turmoil, the conventional rules are suspended, allowing those with the vision and courage to ascend to power. Embracing chaos means recognizing and seizing these moments of disruption to further one's ambitions.

Navigating chaos requires a keen sense of timing and adaptability. One must be able to identify the right moment to act and the best strategy to employ. This ability to thrive in disorder can set you apart as a formidable force.

Harnessing chaos is not about creating disorder for its own sake but about seeing beyond the confusion to the potential gains. By mastering this approach, you can transform seemingly insurmountable challenges into stepping stones to greatness.

## JANUARY 3RD

# THE VALUE OF DECEPTION

*"A well-placed lie is worth a thousand truths."*

Deception, when used judiciously, can be an invaluable tool. It allows one to manipulate reality, create advantageous narratives, and gain the upper hand in various situations. Understanding the art of deception can be a game-changer.

Effective deception requires skill and subtlety. It's about crafting believable lies that serve your purpose while maintaining credibility. This skill can protect you from potential threats and help you achieve your goals without direct confrontation.

The key to successful deception lies in its execution. It should be used sparingly and strategically to avoid long-term consequences. When done right, deception can pave the way for significant achievements and maintain your position of power.

## JANUARY 4TH

# THE STRENGTH OF AMBITION

*"Ambition is the fuel that drives the darkest desires."*

Ambition is a double-edged sword. It can propel you to great heights but also lead you down a morally ambiguous path. Embracing your ambition means acknowledging its potential to shape your destiny, even if it requires stepping over others.

Harnessing ambition involves setting clear, strategic goals and relentlessly pursuing them. It requires a focused mindset and the willingness to make difficult decisions. This relentless drive can set you apart as a leader and innovator.

Balancing ambition with ethics is challenging but necessary. The pursuit of power should not come at the cost of humanity. By channeling ambition positively, you can achieve your desires while maintaining a sense of integrity.

## JANUARY 5TH

# THE ART OF MANIPULATION

*"To manipulate is to shape reality to your will."*

Manipulation is about influencing others to act in ways that serve your interests. It's a skill that, when mastered, can allow you to control outcomes and direct events to your advantage. Understanding the nuances of manipulation can significantly enhance your power.

Effective manipulation involves understanding human nature and motivations. By identifying what drives people, you can craft strategies to influence their actions. This requires emotional intelligence and strategic thinking.

Using manipulation responsibly is essential. The goal is to achieve your objectives without causing undue harm. When practiced ethically, manipulation can be a tool for achieving harmony and order, benefiting both you and those around you.

## JANUARY 6TH

# THE LURE OF POWER

*"Power is the ultimate aphrodisiac."*

Power attracts and influences people, often serving as the ultimate motivator. Those who wield power can shape destinies and create legacies. Recognizing the allure of power is the first step towards understanding how to obtain and use it effectively.

The pursuit of power requires strategic planning, intelligence, and a certain ruthlessness. It's about positioning yourself in the right places, making the right alliances, and sometimes making difficult choices. Power, once attained, must be carefully managed to maintain its hold.

With great power comes great responsibility. It's important to use power judiciously, ensuring that it serves not only your interests but also those of a broader community. True power lies in the ability to influence positively while maintaining control.

## JANUARY 7TH

# THE NECESSITY OF RUTHLESSNESS

*"Kindness is a luxury; ruthlessness is a necessity."*

In a competitive world, ruthlessness often becomes a necessity to achieve one's goals. Kindness, while admirable, can be perceived as a weakness that others may exploit. Understanding the balance between kindness and ruthlessness is crucial for success.

Being ruthless means making tough decisions without being swayed by emotions. It involves prioritizing your goals and sometimes taking actions that may seem harsh. This mindset can prevent others from taking advantage of you and ensure your path to success is unhindered.

However, ruthlessness should be tempered with wisdom. The goal is not to become callous but to be firm and decisive. By mastering the art of ruthlessness, you can protect your interests and navigate the complexities of power dynamics effectively.

## JANUARY 8TH

# THE POWER OF SILENCE

*"Silence speaks louder than words."*

Silence can be a powerful tool in communication. It allows you to observe, listen, and understand more than words ever could. By mastering the art of silence, you can control conversations and gather valuable information.

Using silence strategically can make others uncomfortable, compelling them to reveal more than they intended. It creates a space for contemplation and can convey strength and confidence. Silence can be a form of resistance or a way to assert dominance.

Nevertheless, silence must be used wisely. It's a tool that requires context and timing to be effective. By understanding when to speak and when to remain silent, you can enhance your influence and control over various situations.

## JANUARY 9TH

# THE STRENGTH OF INDEPENDENCE

*"Depend on no one but yourself."*

Independence is a cornerstone of strength. Relying solely on oneself ensures that you remain in control of your destiny and are not vulnerable to the whims of others. Embracing independence means cultivating self-reliance and confidence.

Being independent requires a strong sense of self and the ability to make decisions without external validation. It involves trusting your instincts and taking responsibility for your actions. This autonomy can lead to greater personal and professional success.

True independence doesn't mean isolating oneself. It's about being capable of standing alone while also recognizing the value of strategic alliances. Balancing independence with collaboration can create a powerful foundation for long-term success.

## JANUARY 10TH

# THE UTILITY OF FEARLESSNESS

*"Fear is a cage; break free from it."*

Fear can be paralyzing, preventing you from taking necessary risks and seizing opportunities. Overcoming fear is essential to achieving greatness. Embracing fearlessness means confronting your fears head-on and using them to propel you forward.

Being fearless involves taking calculated risks and stepping out of your comfort zone. It's about pushing boundaries and challenging the status quo. This courage can lead to remarkable achievements and set you apart as a leader.

However, fearlessness must be balanced with prudence. Recklessness can lead to unnecessary risks and failures. By cultivating a fearless yet strategic mindset, you can navigate challenges effectively and achieve your goals with confidence.

## JANUARY 11TH

# THE INFLUENCE OF CHARISMA

*"Charisma is the magic that bends others to your will."*

Charisma is an intangible quality that can greatly enhance your influence over others. It's the ability to attract, charm, and inspire people. Understanding and cultivating charisma can make you a more effective leader and influencer.

Developing charisma involves honing your communication skills, exuding confidence, and being genuinely interested in others. It's about creating a magnetic presence that draws people to you and makes them want to follow your lead.

Charisma, when used wisely, can inspire loyalty and admiration. It's a powerful tool that can help you build strong networks and achieve your objectives. By mastering the art of charisma, you can significantly enhance your ability to shape outcomes and drive success.

## JANUARY 12TH

# THE NECESSITY OF ADAPTABILITY

*"Survival belongs to the adaptable, not the strongest."*

In a constantly changing world, adaptability is key to survival and success. Those who can quickly adjust to new circumstances and challenges are the ones who thrive. Embracing adaptability means being open to change and ready to pivot when necessary.

Being adaptable requires a flexible mindset and a willingness to learn. It's about recognizing when a strategy is no longer working and being willing to change course. This ability to adapt can keep you ahead of the competition and ensure long-term success.

Adaptability should not be confused with inconsistency. It's about making calculated adjustments while maintaining a clear vision and goals. By balancing adaptability with strategic planning, you can navigate uncertainties and emerge stronger.

## JANUARY 13TH

# THE EDGE OF CONFIDENCE

*"Confidence is the armor that shields you from doubt."*

Confidence is a vital attribute for achieving success and maintaining authority. It acts as a protective barrier against self-doubt and external criticism. Embracing confidence means believing in your abilities and decisions, even in the face of challenges.

Building confidence involves self-awareness and continuous improvement. It's about setting realistic goals, celebrating your achievements, and learning from your failures. This internal strength can empower you to take bold actions and pursue your ambitions relentlessly.

Confidence must be tempered with humility. Overconfidence can lead to complacency and mistakes. By balancing confidence with a willingness to learn and adapt, you can maintain a strong, resilient mindset that drives you toward your goals.

## JANUARY 14TH

# THE STRATEGY OF PATIENCE

*"Patience is a weapon; wield it wisely."*

Patience is often undervalued in a world that prizes quick results. However, it is a powerful tool that can lead to more strategic and thoughtful decision-making. Embracing patience means recognizing the value of waiting for the right moment to act.

Being patient involves self-discipline and foresight. It's about understanding that some goals take time to achieve and being willing to wait for the optimal conditions. This approach can prevent rash decisions and lead to more sustainable success.

Patience should not be mistaken for passivity. It's about being active in your preparation and ready to seize opportunities when they arise. By mastering the art of patience, you can make more informed decisions and achieve long-term goals more effectively.

## JANUARY 15TH

# THE ILLUSION OF CONTROL

*"Control the narrative, and you control reality."*

Controlling the narrative means shaping how events and actions are perceived by others. It's a powerful tool for influencing opinions and outcomes. Embracing this concept involves understanding the importance of perception in shaping reality.

Crafting the narrative requires strategic communication and storytelling. It's about presenting information in a way that aligns with your goals and resonates with your audience. This skill can enhance your influence and control over situations.

Controlling the narrative should be done ethically. Manipulating facts can lead to distrust and long-term damage to your reputation. By focusing on truthful yet strategic communication, you can maintain credibility while guiding perceptions in your favor.

## JANUARY 16TH

# THE WEAPON OF KNOWLEDGE

*"Knowledge is power, guard it well."*

Knowledge is one of the most powerful tools at your disposal. It can give you a significant advantage in any situation, enabling you to make informed decisions and anticipate challenges. Embracing the value of knowledge means continuously seeking and safeguarding it.

Acquiring knowledge requires curiosity and a commitment to lifelong learning. It's about staying informed, analyzing information critically, and applying it effectively. This intellectual edge can set you apart as a leader and innovator.

Knowledge must be used wisely and ethically. Hoarding information or using it to deceive others can backfire. By sharing knowledge selectively and responsibly, you can build trust and enhance your influence while maintaining your strategic advantage.

## January 17th

# The Virtue of Cunning

*"Cunning is the art of winning without fighting."*

Cunning is about using intelligence and strategy to achieve your goals without direct confrontation. It involves outthinking and outmaneuvering your opponents. Embracing cunning means recognizing the value of subtlety and strategy in overcoming obstacles.

Being cunning requires mental agility and foresight. It's about anticipating challenges and devising creative solutions. This approach can help you avoid unnecessary conflicts and achieve your objectives more efficiently.

However, cunning must be balanced with integrity. Deception and manipulation can damage relationships and reputations. By using cunning ethically, you can navigate challenges smartly while maintaining trust and respect.

## JANUARY 18TH

# THE REALITY OF SACRIFICE

*"Greatness demands sacrifice."*

Achieving greatness often requires significant sacrifices. It's about prioritizing long-term goals over immediate gratification and being willing to give up certain comforts. Embracing sacrifice means recognizing its role in the journey to success.

Making sacrifices involves tough choices and a clear vision of your goals. It's about understanding what you're willing to give up to achieve something greater. This commitment can lead to remarkable achievements and set you apart as a dedicated individual.

Remember that sacrifice should be made thoughtfully. It's important to weigh the potential benefits against the costs and ensure that your sacrifices align with your values and long-term objectives. By making strategic sacrifices, you can pave the way for sustained success.

## JANUARY 19TH

# THE INFLUENCE OF PERSUASION

*"Persuasion is the key to bending others to your will."*

Persuasion is a powerful tool for influencing others and achieving your goals. It's about convincing people to see things from your perspective and act in ways that benefit you. Understanding the art of persuasion can significantly enhance your ability to shape outcomes.

Effective persuasion requires empathy and strategic communication. It's about understanding the needs and motivations of others and framing your arguments in a way that resonates with them. This skill can help you build alliances and achieve your objectives more smoothly.

Persuasion should be used ethically. Manipulating others for selfish reasons can lead to distrust and backlash. By focusing on win-win scenarios and being honest in your intentions, you can use persuasion to create positive outcomes for all parties involved.

## JANUARY 20TH

# THE ROLE OF RESILIENCE

*"Resilience is the strength to rise after every fall."*

Resilience is the ability to bounce back from setbacks and keep moving forward. It's about maintaining your determination and focus despite challenges. Embracing resilience means recognizing its importance in achieving long-term success.

Building resilience involves developing a positive mindset and learning from failures. It's about seeing obstacles as opportunities for growth and being persistent in your efforts. This tenacity can help you overcome difficulties and reach your goals.

Resilience should not be confused with stubbornness. It's about being adaptable and willing to change your approach when necessary. By balancing resilience with flexibility, you can navigate challenges more effectively and achieve sustained success.

## JANUARY 21ST

# THE IMPACT OF INFLUENCE

*"Influence is more potent than authority."*

Influence is the ability to shape others' actions and decisions through subtle guidance rather than direct control. It's about earning respect and trust, which allows you to lead without force. Embracing influence means understanding its power and how to wield it effectively.

Building influence requires strong relationships and a deep understanding of human nature. It's about connecting with people on a personal level and demonstrating competence and integrity. This approach can help you achieve your goals through collaboration and mutual respect.

Influence must be used responsibly. Manipulating others for personal gain can lead to resentment and loss of trust. By using your influence to inspire and uplift, you can create positive and lasting impacts on those around you.

## JANUARY 22ND

# THE STRATEGY OF SECRECY

*"Secrets are the currency of power."*

Secrets hold significant power, providing leverage and protection in various situations. Controlling information and deciding when and how to reveal it can be a strategic advantage. Embracing secrecy means recognizing its value in maintaining power and influence.

Maintaining secrecy requires discretion and careful judgment. It's about knowing which information to share and which to withhold. This skill can help you navigate complex social and professional landscapes, ensuring that you stay ahead of the competition.

However, secrecy must be balanced with transparency. Being overly secretive can lead to mistrust and isolation. By sharing information strategically and responsibly, you can build trust while retaining your strategic advantage.

# THE COMMAND OF PRESENCE

*"Presence is the silent power that commands respect."*

Presence is about how you carry yourself and the impression you leave on others. It's a combination of confidence, charisma, and authenticity that commands respect and attention. Embracing your presence means recognizing its impact and cultivating it intentionally.

Developing a commanding presence involves self-awareness and continuous self-improvement. It's about exuding confidence and being genuine in your interactions. This authenticity can help you build strong connections and establish authority naturally.

Presence should be cultivated with humility. It's not about seeking attention for its own sake but about using your influence to create positive change. By balancing presence with empathy and integrity, you can lead effectively and inspire others.

## JANUARY 24TH

# THE EDGE OF AMBIGUITY

*"Ambiguity is a weapon; use it to keep others guessing."*

Ambiguity can be a strategic tool for maintaining control and keeping others uncertain about your intentions. It allows you to maneuver flexibly and keep your opponents off balance. Embracing ambiguity means understanding its potential to create strategic advantages.

Using ambiguity effectively requires skillful communication and a deep understanding of context. It's about being deliberately vague when necessary and providing clarity when it serves your purpose. This approach can help you protect your plans and adapt to changing circumstances.

However, ambiguity must be used sparingly and ethically. Overuse can lead to confusion and mistrust. By balancing ambiguity with transparency, you can maintain control while ensuring that you build trust and credibility with those who matter.

## JANUARY 25TH

# THE VIRTUE OF PERSISTENCE

*"Persistence wears down resistance."*

Persistence is about unwavering determination and the ability to keep pushing forward despite obstacles. It's a powerful attribute that can overcome resistance and lead to success. Embracing persistence means recognizing its role in achieving long-term goals.

Building persistence involves setting clear goals and maintaining focus even when faced with setbacks. It's about seeing challenges as temporary and believing in your ability to overcome them. This resilience can help you achieve your ambitions and stand out as a dedicated individual.

Persistence must be balanced with adaptability. It's important to know when to change your approach or pivot your strategy. By combining persistence with flexibility, you can navigate obstacles more effectively and achieve sustained success.

## JANUARY 26TH

# THE WISDOM OF PATIENCE

*"Patience is the art of hiding your claws."*

Patience involves waiting for the right moment to strike, allowing you to gather information and assess the situation before acting. It's a strategic approach that can lead to more effective and decisive actions. Embracing patience means recognizing its value in achieving your goals.

Developing patience requires self-discipline and a long-term perspective. It's about staying calm and composed, even in challenging situations, and waiting for the opportune moment to act. This approach can prevent rash decisions and lead to more successful outcomes.

Patience must be combined with readiness. It's about being prepared to act when the time is right, rather than simply waiting passively. By mastering the art of patience, you can make more strategic decisions and achieve your goals more effectively.

## JANUARY 27TH

# THE POWER OF VISION

*"Vision is the light that guides you through darkness."*

A clear vision provides direction and purpose, helping you navigate challenges and stay focused on your goals. It's a powerful motivator that can inspire you and others to achieve great things. Embracing vision means recognizing its importance in shaping your future.

Developing a vision involves setting clear, achievable goals and creating a roadmap to reach them. It's about understanding your strengths and weaknesses and leveraging them effectively. This clarity can help you stay motivated and overcome obstacles more easily.

Vision must be balanced with practicality. It's important to be realistic about your capabilities and resources and to adjust your plans as necessary. By combining vision with strategic planning, you can achieve your goals more effectively and create a lasting impact.

# THE IMPACT OF AUTHORITY

*"Authority commands respect; use it wisely."*

Authority is the legitimate power to influence others and make decisions. It's a crucial aspect of leadership that can inspire respect and obedience. Embracing authority means understanding its responsibilities and using it to achieve positive outcomes.

Building authority involves demonstrating competence, integrity, and fairness. It's about earning respect through your actions and decisions. This approach can help you establish a strong, credible presence and lead more effectively.

Authority should be exercised with humility and empathy. It's important to listen to others and consider their perspectives. By balancing authority with compassion, you can create a positive and inclusive environment that fosters trust and cooperation.

## JANUARY 29TH

# THE ROLE OF STRATEGY

*"Strategy is the blueprint of victory."*

Strategy is about planning and executing actions to achieve specific goals. It's a critical component of success that involves careful analysis and foresight. Embracing strategy means recognizing its importance in guiding your actions and decisions.

Developing a strategy requires understanding your objectives, resources, and potential challenges. It's about creating a plan that leverages your strengths and mitigates your weaknesses. This approach can help you achieve your goals more efficiently and effectively.

However, strategy must be adaptable. It's important to be flexible and willing to adjust your plans as circumstances change. By combining strategic planning with adaptability, you can navigate uncertainties and achieve sustained success.

## JANUARY 30TH

# THE POWER OF INFLUENCE

*"Influence is the silent force that shapes the world."*

Influence is the ability to affect others' thoughts, feelings, and actions. It's a subtle yet powerful force that can shape outcomes and drive change. Embracing influence means understanding its potential and how to use it effectively.

Building influence requires strong relationships and effective communication. It's about connecting with people on a personal level and understanding their needs and motivations. This approach can help you inspire and lead others more effectively.

Remember that influence must be used ethically. Manipulating others for personal gain can lead to distrust and resentment. By using your influence to create positive change and build trust, you can achieve your goals while maintaining strong, supportive relationships.

## JANUARY 31ST

# THE POWER OF RESILIENCE

*"Resilience is the backbone of the powerful."*

Resilience is the capacity to recover from setbacks and keep moving forward. It is essential for anyone striving to achieve greatness, as it allows you to withstand and overcome obstacles. Embracing resilience means recognizing its importance in enduring the journey toward success.

Cultivating resilience involves developing a positive mindset and a strong support system. It's about viewing challenges as opportunities to grow and learning from failures. This perspective can help you stay motivated and persistent in pursuing your goals.

Resilience must be balanced with self-care. It's important to take breaks and recharge to maintain your strength and focus. By combining resilience with a healthy lifestyle, you can sustain your efforts and achieve your goals more effectively.

# FEBRUARY

## FEBRUARY 1ST

# THE ART OF STRATEGY

*"Strategy is the silent war of the mind."*

Strategy involves planning and executing actions to achieve specific goals. It requires careful analysis, foresight, and adaptability. Embracing strategy means recognizing its role in navigating complex situations and achieving success.

Developing a strategy requires understanding your objectives, resources, and potential challenges. It's about creating a plan that leverages your strengths and mitigates your weaknesses. This approach can help you achieve your goals more efficiently and effectively.

However, strategy must be adaptable. Circumstances change, and being willing to adjust your plans is crucial. By combining strategic planning with flexibility, you can navigate uncertainties and achieve sustained success.

## FEBRUARY 2ND

# THE POWER OF LUST

*"Lust is the fervent passion that drives relentless pursuit, transforming desire into a relentless force for achievement."*

Tap into the intense energy of lust to fuel your ambitions. View your goals not just as distant dreams but as tantalizing desires that must be fulfilled. Lust is more than a mere craving; it is a driving force that can propel you forward, breaking through barriers with sheer determination. Embrace this fervent passion and allow it to infuse every aspect of your life, pushing you to pursue your objectives with an unyielding vigor.

Focus this passionate drive on your objectives, turning every obstacle into a challenge to overcome. Lust for success can transform daunting barriers into stepping stones on your path to greatness. Harnessed correctly, it becomes a powerful catalyst for achieving the impossible. Let your lust fuel your relentless pursuit of excellence.

Using the power of lust, transform your deepest desires into your greatest strengths. Directed with precision and purpose, lust can lead to extraordinary achievements. It becomes a fundamental part of your identity, driving you to reach heights you never thought possible. Channel this energy wisely, turning your desires from dreams into attainable realities.

## FEBRUARY 3RD

# THE POWER OF ADAPTABILITY

*"Adaptability is the strength to bend without breaking."*

Adaptability is the ability to adjust to new circumstances and challenges. It is essential for survival and success in a constantly changing world. Embracing adaptability means being open to change and ready to pivot when necessary.

Being adaptable requires a flexible mindset and a willingness to learn. It's about recognizing when a strategy is no longer working and being willing to change course. This ability to adapt can keep you ahead of the competition and ensure long-term success.

Adaptability should not be confused with inconsistency. It's about making calculated adjustments while maintaining a clear vision and goals. By balancing adaptability with strategic planning, you can navigate uncertainties and emerge stronger.

**FEBRUARY 4TH**

# THE STRENGTH OF POWER

*"Power is the leverage that shapes destinies, wielded with precision to bend the world to your will."*

Understand that power is the ultimate tool for achieving your goals. With power, you can influence, control, and direct outcomes to your advantage. The pursuit of power is not merely about dominance but about shaping the world around you to fit your vision. Look at political leaders and influential figures who use their authority to implement policies and reforms, changing the course of history. Power, when wielded with precision, can be a transformative force.

Build your strength through alliances, strategic moves, and unwavering resolve. Power isn't just brute force but strategic use of influence. Form alliances, enhance your authority, and maintain unshakable resolve. Each step should increase your power and extend your influence, ensuring control of your destiny.

Use power wisely to maintain stability and achieve your vision. Effective power transforms not just your destiny but those around you. Use it responsibly to ensure positive, lasting change. By mastering power, you shape the world to your will, achieve your objectives, and leave a lasting impact.

## FEBRUARY 5TH

# THE RESOLVE OF VENGEANCE

*"Vengeance is the fire that consumes until justice is served, turning past wrongs into future triumphs."*

Let vengeance fuel your actions by viewing every slight and betrayal as a catalyst for your rise. Vengeance can be a powerful motivator, driving you to seek retribution and justice for past wrongs. Channel your desire for retribution into meticulously planned actions that address grievances. Think of the betrayed business partner who strategically dismantles the empire of their traitorous associate. Vengeance, when directed properly, can transform pain into power.

Use your sense of justice to drive you forward, ensuring your revenge is both satisfying and effective. Vengeance should be about calculated, precise actions that achieve your desired outcome. Each move should be part of a strategy to reclaim power and ensure those who wronged you face consequences. This methodical approach ensures vengeance serves as both retribution and a means to elevate yourself.

When executed with precision and patience, vengeance can turn your greatest pain into triumph. It becomes a journey of transformation, where each act of retribution brings you closer to your goals. Let your resolve be unyielding, using vengeance to fuel your ascent. Turning past wrongs into future successes will define your strength and determination.

## FEBRUARY 6TH

# THE SCENT OF BETRAYAL

*"Betrayal has a distinct scent, intoxicating and potent,
leading the way to unassailable power."*

Betrayal is the perfume of the cunning, an intoxicating aroma that lingers long after the act is done. It is the hidden dagger, the secret smile, the whisper in the night that shatters alliances and crumbles empires. Embracing betrayal means understanding that loyalty is a fickle currency, easily spent and rarely returned. In the game of power, trust is but an illusion, and those who master betrayal wield it as their greatest weapon.

When you embrace your inner villain, you learn that betrayal is not a sign of weakness but a demonstration of supreme strength. It is the ultimate test of character, separating the wolves from the sheep. Those who dare to betray are not bound by the petty morals of the common man; they see the world for what it truly is—a battlefield where only the most ruthless survive. So, inhale deeply, savor the scent of betrayal, and let it guide you to unassailable power.

## FEBRUARY 7TH

# THE ROLE OF CHARISMA

*"Charisma is the invisible force that draws
others in."*

Charisma is an intangible quality that can greatly enhance your influence over others. It's the ability to attract, charm, and inspire people. Understanding and cultivating charisma can make you a more effective leader and influencer.

Developing charisma involves honing your communication skills, exuding confidence, and being genuinely interested in others. It's about creating a magnetic presence that draws people to you and makes them want to follow your lead.

Charisma, when used wisely, can inspire loyalty and admiration. It's a powerful tool that can help you build strong networks and achieve your objectives. By mastering the art of charisma, you can significantly enhance your ability to shape outcomes and drive success.

## FEBRUARY 8TH

# THE SHADOW OF CRUELTY

*"Cruelty casts a long shadow, under which power flourishes and rivals wither."*

Cruelty is the shadow that envelops the strong, a dark veil under which power flourishes and rivals wither. It is the cold, calculated act that instills fear and commands respect. Embracing cruelty means abandoning the pretense of kindness and embracing the stark reality that only the ruthless truly thrive. It is the sharp blade of truth in a world of comforting lies.

In the embrace of your inner villain, you will discover that cruelty is not merely an act but a state of being. It is the willingness to do what others will not, to cross lines they dare not approach. Under the shadow of cruelty, your power will grow, and those who oppose you will find their strength sapped, their resolve shattered. Let cruelty be your guide, your weapon, and your shield as you carve your name into the annals of history.

## FEBRUARY 9TH

# THE PULSE OF AMBITION

*"Ambition pulses through the veins, fueling the heart's darkest desires and the mind's most ruthless plans."*

Ambition is the lifeblood of the villainous heart, a pulsing force that fuels the darkest desires and the most ruthless plans. It is the relentless drive that refuses to be satisfied with mediocrity, the insatiable thirst for power and influence. Embracing ambition means acknowledging that there are no limits, no moral boundaries that cannot be crossed in the pursuit of greatness.

As you embrace your inner villain, you will come to see ambition as your greatest ally. It is the unyielding force that propels you forward, the burning desire that keeps you awake at night plotting your next move. Ambition is not a sin but a virtue, the mark of those destined for greatness. Let it pulse through your veins, let it fuel your every action, and let it drive you to achieve the impossible.

**FEBRUARY 10TH**

# THE WISDOM OF GREED

*"Greed is the fuel that ignites the quest for more, turning insatiable desire into boundless opportunity."*

Use greed as a powerful motivator to drive you to new heights. In the world of ambition, greed is often seen as a negative trait, but when harnessed correctly, it can be a force of incredible potential. Every aspiration becomes a stepping stone to greater wealth, power, and success. Your insatiable desire for more can push you to explore new ventures and seek out opportunities that others might overlook, making your path to success even clearer.

View every situation as a chance to expand your influence and resources. Like a master entrepreneur, seek new ventures and exploit overlooked opportunities. Greed, balanced with strategy and ethics, drives relentless and effective ambition. This pursuit is a calculated approach to growth and success, not recklessness.

Channel your greed strategically to drive your ambitions, ensuring your pursuit is ethical and beneficial in the long term. Greed, when viewed through ambition and opportunity, becomes a powerful engine of success. It drives you to never settle, always seek more, and push boundaries. Let greed turn your insatiable desires into boundless opportunities.

## FEBRUARY 11TH

# THE ALLURE OF NARCISSISM

*"Narcissism is the mirror that reflects boundless self-worth, turning self-love into a source of power."*

Recognize the strength in narcissism by letting your self-confidence and belief in your own importance drive you to assert your dominance. When harnessed correctly, narcissism can be a powerful motivator. Use your charm and charisma to captivate and influence those around you. Imagine a celebrity who constantly promotes their brand, ensuring they remain in the public eye. Project unshakable self-assurance, drawing others to you and using your self-love as a foundation for your rise to power.

Narcissism allows you to project confidence and authority, attracting others to your cause. This self-assuredness can be contagious, inspiring loyalty and admiration from those around you. By cultivating your image and maintaining a strong sense of self, you can create an aura of invincibility that draws people in and keeps them aligned with your goals.

When balanced with strategy, narcissism can be a powerful force for achieving your ambitions. Temper self-love with clear vision and ethics to avoid alienating supporters. Mastering the allure of narcissism allows you to leverage confidence and charisma, building a loyal following and achieving your objectives with unwavering support.

# THE CRAFT OF DECEIT

*"Deceit is the art that veils the truth for gain, turning reality into a canvas of your own making."*

Perfect the craft of deceit by understanding that truth is malleable and can be shaped to serve your purposes. Deceit isn't just about lying but creating a reality that works to your advantage. Use misinformation and strategic lies to create beneficial illusions and manipulate perceptions. Like a master spy gathering intelligence and manipulating events, skillful deceit can be a powerful tool in your arsenal.

Craft your deceptions carefully to achieve desired outcomes. Deceit requires understanding human nature and psychology. Each lie should be a well-constructed part of your strategy. By mastering deceit, you can control narratives, influence decisions, and achieve goals with subtlety.

In a world where appearances often matter more than reality, mastering deceit makes you formidable. Use this power sparingly and with precision, as overuse can lead to downfall. Employ deceit wisely to navigate complex scenarios and achieve your ambitions, always aware of potential consequences and ready to adapt.

## FEBRUARY 13TH

# THE BLADE OF DETERMINATION

*"Determination is the blade that slices through barriers,
carving a path of relentless resolve."*

Adopt a ruthless determination to achieve your goals, understanding that in the pursuit of greatness, there is no room for hesitation or mercy. Ruthlessness is about having the clarity and conviction to make tough decisions and take decisive actions. Approach each challenge with a cold, calculated mindset, making tough decisions others shy away from. Consider the cutthroat CEO who ensures the company's survival and growth through difficult choices. Strategic ruthlessness can pave the way to unparalleled success.

Let your resolve be as sharp as a blade, cutting through any obstacle. Each decision and action should focus on achieving your objectives. This unwavering determination allows you to push forward relentlessly, regardless of difficulties. By embracing ruthlessness, you ensure nothing diverts you from your path, maintaining a clear focus on your end goals.

Balance ambition with the cold efficiency needed to reach your goals. By mastering ruthless determination, you can achieve your objectives and carve a path to greatness, overcoming obstacles with ease and precision.

# THE TASTE OF GREED

*"Greed leaves a lingering taste, one that grows sweeter with each indulgence and every conquest."*

Greed is the flavor that fuels the fire within, a sweet nectar that grows ever more tantalizing with each indulgence. It is the relentless drive that propels the ambitious forward, the insatiable hunger that cannot be sated by mere wealth or power. Embracing greed means casting aside the chains of contentment and striving for more—more influence, more control, more of everything that sets you apart from the ordinary.

As you delve deeper into your inner villain, you will find that greed is not a vice but a virtue. It is the essence of true ambition, the spark that ignites revolutions and topples kings. Each conquest, each acquisition, only sharpens the taste, making the next goal even more irresistible. So, savor the taste of greed, let it linger on your tongue, and let it drive you to conquer worlds and bend them to your will.

## February 15th

# The Pleasure of Cruelty

*"Cruelty is the pleasure derived from exerting power over others, turning fear into a tool of control."*

Find strength in cruelty by recognizing that fear is a powerful motivator. Cruelty, when applied judiciously, can be a tool for maintaining control and ensuring compliance. Consider a ruthless dictator who instills fear to keep order and prevent rebellion. Use calculated cruelty to maintain control and ensure compliance. Exercise your power with precision, ensuring your dominance is unquestioned.

Cruelty should be used sparingly and strategically, as a means to an end rather than an end in itself. The key is to instill enough fear to maintain control without causing unnecessary rebellion. By wielding cruelty with care, you can create an environment where your authority remains unchallenged and your power is absolute.

Use cruelty sparingly to avoid inciting unnecessary rebellion and maintain your rule. When applied correctly, cruelty can ensure that your commands are followed and your authority is respected. By understanding and harnessing the pleasure of cruelty, you can maintain a firm grip on power, using fear as your ultimate tool for control and ensuring that your rule is both effective and unchallenged.

**FEBRUARY 16TH**

# THE STRENGTH OF RUTHLESSNESS

*"Ruthlessness is the edge that cuts through weakness."*

In a competitive world, ruthlessness often becomes a necessity to achieve one's goals. Kindness, while admirable, can be perceived as a weakness that others may exploit. Understanding the balance between kindness and ruthlessness is crucial for success.

Being ruthless means making tough decisions without being swayed by emotions. It involves prioritizing your goals and sometimes taking actions that may seem harsh. This mindset can prevent others from taking advantage of you and ensure your path to success is unhindered.

Ruthlessness should be tempered with wisdom and ethics. It's important not to become callous or unjust in your actions. By balancing ruthlessness with fairness and integrity, you can maintain respect and achieve long-term success.

## FEBRUARY 17TH

# THE EDGE OF SELF-BELIEF

*"Self-belief is the foundation of all achievements."*

Self-belief is the cornerstone of all success. It is the unwavering confidence in your abilities and potential. Without self-belief, even the best-laid plans can falter. Embracing self-belief means trusting yourself and your capabilities, regardless of external circumstances.

Building self-belief involves recognizing your strengths and accomplishments, setting realistic goals, and persevering through challenges. It's about maintaining a positive self-image and refusing to be discouraged by setbacks. This inner confidence can drive you to achieve your highest aspirations.

Self-belief should be balanced with self-awareness. It's important to recognize your limitations and be open to feedback and growth. By combining self-belief with a willingness to learn and improve, you can achieve sustained success and fulfillment.

# THE ART OF PERSUASION

*"Persuasion is the art of bending others to your will."*

Persuasion is a powerful tool for influencing others and achieving your goals. It's about convincing people to see things from your perspective and act in ways that benefit you. Understanding the art of persuasion can significantly enhance your ability to shape outcomes.

Effective persuasion requires empathy and strategic communication. It's about understanding the needs and motivations of others and framing your arguments in a way that resonates with them. This skill can help you build alliances and achieve your objectives more smoothly.

However, persuasion should be used ethically. Manipulating others for selfish reasons can lead to distrust and backlash. By focusing on win-win scenarios and being honest in your intentions, you can use persuasion to create positive outcomes for all parties involved.

## FEBRUARY 19TH

# THE ESSENCE OF FEARLESSNESS

*"Fearlessness is the courage to face the unknown."*

Fearlessness is the quality of confronting challenges and uncertainties without being paralyzed by fear. It's about having the courage to take risks and pursue your goals despite potential obstacles. Embracing fearlessness means recognizing its importance in achieving greatness.

Cultivating fearlessness involves building self-confidence and a positive mindset. It's about seeing fear as a natural part of growth and learning to push through it. This resilience can help you tackle challenges head-on and achieve your aspirations.

Fearlessness should be balanced with caution. It's important to assess risks carefully and make informed decisions. By combining fearlessness with strategic planning, you can navigate uncertainties more effectively and achieve lasting success.

# THE ART OF MASTERY

*"Mastery is not about doing extraordinary things, but about doing ordinary things extraordinarily well."*

Mastery in any field involves tapping into the deeper, often darker parts of our psyche that drive us to excel beyond the ordinary. It's about channeling our innermost ambitions and desires into a relentless pursuit of excellence. This path is not just about refining skills but about embracing the parts of ourselves that are ruthlessly dedicated to achieving greatness, regardless of the obstacles.

This journey requires an intimate understanding of one's own strengths and weaknesses, often pushing moral and ethical boundaries to test how far one is willing to go for success. It's about recognizing that the shadows within us—our fears, our obsessions—are powerful motivators that, when harnessed, can propel us to levels of achievement we never thought possible.

Mastery is not achieved in isolation. It influences and intimidates, setting a standard that challenges others to either rise to our level or remain in our shadow. By accepting and mastering the darker parts of your character, you not only excel in your pursuits but also shape the environment around you, often dictating the pace and direction of others' ambitions.

# THE TEMPTATION OF POWER

*"Power tempts even the strongest of wills."*

The allure of power is inherently linked to the darker facets of human nature. It speaks to a deep-seated desire to control and influence, often overriding moral constraints in favor of personal gain. Embracing this aspect of power means acknowledging and wielding these darker impulses responsibly, using them to assert dominance and achieve strategic advantages.

Power, when embraced with full awareness of its corruptive potential, can be a formidable tool. It allows one to navigate and manipulate the dynamics of any situation to one's favor, often bending others' wills subtly without open coercion. This subtle art of control is a hallmark of those who have mastered their inner villain, turning potential threats into opportunities.

The exercise of power must be balanced with cunning and restraint. Too overt a display can breed resistance, while too subtle may be ineffectual. The true villain knows the precise amount of pressure to apply, ensuring their influence is felt but not so visible as to incite backlash.

# THE SHADOWS OF DOUBT

*"Doubt casts long shadows over the bravest intentions."*

Doubt serves the inner villain by acting as a tool for introspection and strategy. It forces us to question not just our plans but also our motivations, pushing us to consider more cunning, less straightforward paths to our goals. Embracing doubt means acknowledging the darker uncertainties within us that challenge the status quo and provoke deeper thinking.

In the realm of strategic manipulation, doubt can be weaponized to undermine opponents and strengthen one's position. It involves planting seeds of uncertainty, leading others to falter under their own questioning. For the master strategist, doubt is not a weakness but a weapon, refined and honed to destabilize the confident and control the narrative.

Successfully navigating through doubt requires a keen awareness of one's darker nature and an understanding of how to leverage it. This includes using doubt to refine your tactics and emerge more formidable, ensuring that each step taken is done so with deliberate intent and savage efficiency.

## FEBRUARY 23RD

# THE DANCE OF DECEPTION

*"Deception is a dance best performed in the shadows."*

Deception is a vital component of any villain's arsenal. It's about understanding and manipulating perceptions, crafting illusions that serve to advance hidden agendas. Embracing deception means not just accepting but reveling in one's ability to distort reality in ways that serve one's darker purposes.

This dance involves knowing when to hide and when to reveal, mastering the art of misdirection to keep others off-balance and reactive. It requires a deep understanding of human psychology, exploiting weaknesses and desires to bend others to your will. The true artistry of deception lies not in mere trickery, but in transforming it into a form of dark control, guiding others down a path they believe to be of their own choosing.

Effective deception demands a level of self-awareness and control that many fail to achieve. It involves not only deceiving others but also managing one's own darker impulses, ensuring that every lie and every truth is a calculated move in a larger, more sinister strategy.

**FEBRUARY 24TH**

# THE ECHOES OF AMBITION

*"Ambition's echoes resonate long after actions fade."*

Ambition, when fueled by the darker parts of our nature, can drive us to pursue power and success with a relentless fervor. This type of ambition is not satisfied with mere achievement; it thrives on the conquest, on the assertion of dominance over others. Embracing this shadowy drive means recognizing and utilizing the less savory aspects of your character to push forward your agenda.

Such ambition often leads one down paths less trodden, where the rules are bent and morals are flexible. It involves a Machiavellian approach to goals, where the ends often justify the means. By acknowledging and channeling this darker form of ambition, you not only achieve your desires but also imprint your will on the world around you, often leaving a legacy that is both feared and admired.

This darker ambition can serve as a powerful motivator for others, inspiring awe and dread in equal measure. It is not merely about achieving success but about reshaping the landscape of power and influence, often at the expense of others. This is the echo of true ambition—the sound of barriers breaking and wills bending to the force of your darker nature.

## FEBRUARY 25TH

# THE LABYRINTH OF MANIPULATION

*"Within every truth lies a labyrinth of deceit."*

Manipulation is a dark art, skillfully navigating between shades of truth and deception. Embracing this aspect means understanding that every truth can serve as a tool for manipulation, twisted just enough to serve darker purposes. This requires a sophisticated understanding of how facts are perceived and the ability to mold those perceptions to fit your strategic ends.

Mastering manipulation involves more than just lying; it involves creating a version of reality that others are inclined to believe and follow. It's about weaving a web in which others become entangled, often without their knowledge. The true power in manipulation lies not just in deceiving others but in convincing them that they are still in control of their choices and actions.

Manipulation, when executed with finesse, can be imperceptible, even to the most discerning eye. It requires a careful balance of giving and withholding information, leading others down a path they think they have chosen themselves. This method ensures that your influence is both deep and hidden, allowing you to shape outcomes subtly yet profoundly.

**FEBRUARY 26TH**

# THE ALLURE OF SHADOWS

*"Shadows are not merely absence of light; they are
sanctuaries for those who wield darkness."*

The allure of shadows lies in their mystery and the power they confer to those who understand their depths. Embracing the shadows means recognizing your darker impulses and using them as a refuge and a source of strength. Shadows provide cover for actions that might otherwise be scrutinized, allowing the inner villain to operate with freedom and discretion.

Utilizing the shadows effectively requires an acceptance of one's darker side and the ability to navigate through moral ambiguities with ease. It's about finding comfort in the unseen, where strategies can be developed without the interference of societal norms and judgments. Shadows are not just hiding places but strategic bases from which to influence and expand power discreetly.

Shadows offer a canvas on which the nuances of manipulation, control, and ambition can be practiced without restraint. For those who embrace their inner villain, shadows are not ominous; they are opportunities. They are where plans are crafted, where the future is shaped, and where true influence lies dormant, waiting to be unleashed.

## FEBRUARY 27TH

# THE CURRENCY OF SECRETS

*"Secrets are the currency of the wise, spent only when the price is right."*

In the economy of power, secrets are invaluable assets. Understanding and leveraging secrets means recognizing their potential to change the balance of power and using them judiciously. This requires a keen sense of timing and the ability to discern when a secret can yield the highest dividends. Embracing this darker impulse involves not just keeping secrets, but knowing when to reveal them for maximum impact.

Secrets hold power because they contain the unknown—information that can shift perceptions and influence outcomes. The wise villain collects secrets not merely for the sake of knowledge but as leverage. Each secret is a potential move in the complex chess game of power dynamics, where the right revelation can checkmate an opponent.

The handling of secrets demands a strategic mind and an iron will. The temptation to reveal what you know can be overwhelming, but the true master of secrets understands that their value often increases with time. Patience, then, becomes a critical component of using secrets effectively, ensuring that when they are finally used, they are worth more than their weight in gold.

**FEBRUARY 28TH**

# THE SEDUCTION OF POWER

*"Power seduces the strongest minds; it is the ultimate test of character."*

Power is inherently seductive and intoxicating, often seen as the ultimate prize in the games of ambition and control. To embrace the seduction of power is to understand its nature fully—its ability to corrupt, to blind, and to transform. This awareness allows those who seek power to use it not just as a means to an end but as a tool for greater influence and domination.

The path to power is fraught with temptations and risks, requiring a balance between desire for authority and its responsibilities. The inner villain thrives on this challenge, forging a formidable and respected persona. Power tests character, revealing leadership through cruelty or cunning, an iron fist or a manipulative touch.

Maintaining power involves constant vigilance, strategic planning, and occasional ruthlessness. It requires understanding human nature and anticipating rivals' moves. For those adept in darker arts, power is not just a goal but a canvas, painting their legacy with strokes of fear and admiration.

## February 29th

# The Paradox of Control

*"Control is an illusion, masterfully painted by the skilled."*

The desire for control is a fundamental aspect of our darker nature, driving us to manipulate situations to our advantage. True control, however, is not about overt domination but about understanding the subtleties of influence. Embracing this paradox means using your inner villain to orchestrate outcomes behind the scenes, allowing others to believe they are in charge while you pull the strings discreetly.

Control in this sense becomes an art form, requiring a deep understanding of human behavior and strategic foresight. It's about setting the stage, guiding pieces into place without revealing the hand that moves them. This shadowy approach not only ensures compliance but also fosters a sense of autonomy in your pawns, making them unwitting allies in your schemes.

Mastering this illusion requires patience and precision. The most effective villains know that true control is about balance—too little and you risk chaos; too much, and you may provoke rebellion. By finely tuning their approach, they maintain dominance without appearing as tyrants, manipulating from the shadows and ensuring their influence is both pervasive and hidden.

# MARCH

## MARCH 1ST

# THE INTRIGUE OF AMBIGUITY

*"Clarity is the refuge of the mundane; ambiguity, the sanctuary of the insightful."*

Ambiguity offers a strategic advantage, allowing the inner villain to remain elusive and unpredictable. Embracing ambiguity means mastering the art of revealing just enough to keep others engaged but not enough to unveil your plans. This tactic confuses and fascinates, drawing others into a web of intrigue that you control.

The power of ambiguity lies in its ability to make others question their assumptions and second-guess their strategies. It creates a smokescreen where motives are hidden and actions can be disguised. This allows you to maneuver freely, adjusting your tactics as the situation evolves without revealing your true intentions.

Utilizing ambiguity enhances your mystique and power, making you a figure of speculation and respect. By keeping your adversaries and allies alike guessing, you maintain the upper hand. The effective use of ambiguity demands a keen intellect and a deep understanding of the psychological play involved in relationships of power. For those skilled in the dark arts, ambiguity is not just a defense mechanism but an offensive strategy that keeps opponents off balance and under control.

## MARCH 2ND

# THE MASTERY OF MISDIRECTION

*"Look here, while I operate there; the essence of all strategy is misdirection."*

Misdirection is a key strategy in the arsenal of any skilled manipulator. It involves directing attention away from your true actions or intentions, allowing you to execute your plans unnoticed. Embracing this darker tactic means understanding the art of distraction and deception, turning the focus of others towards irrelevant details while you advance your true agenda.

The successful use of misdirection requires creativity and cunning. It is about orchestrating a spectacle that captivates and mesmerizes, making the insignificant seem important. This strategy is often used in politics, business, and even personal relationships, where steering the narrative can lead to control over outcomes.

Mastering misdirection allows you to operate with a degree of freedom that straightforward tactics do not permit. By confusing or diluting the perceptions of others, you create a protective veil for your activities. This not only safeguards your plans but also enhances your reputation as an enigmatic and formidable player in any field.

## MARCH 3RD

# THE VEIL OF SECRECY

*"Under the veil of secrecy, the darkest plans flourish."*

Secrecy is a fundamental element in plotting any significant action that requires discretion and surprise. Embracing the veil of secrecy means not just keeping your strategies hidden but also cultivating a climate of confidentiality that protects all your endeavors. This approach is crucial when navigating environments where the stakes are high and the margins for error are low.

The cultivation of secrecy involves more than just not divulging information; it's about creating layers of misdirection and ambiguity around your actions. It requires building trust and loyalty among those within your inner circle, ensuring that leaks are minimized and that every participant understands the value of discretion.

The power of secrecy lies in its ability to shield your moves from prying eyes, allowing you to build momentum quietly until your plans are unstoppable. It turns your agenda into a fortress, guarded not just by silence but by the active obfuscation of your true intentions. For those who master it, secrecy is not merely a defensive tactic but a weapon of choice.

## MARCH 4TH

# THE ALLURE OF DARKNESS

*"Darkness is not merely the absence of light but a shroud for the cunning."*

The allure of darkness lies in its ability to hide and obscure, providing a perfect backdrop for those who operate best out of sight. Embracing this element of your darker side means recognizing the advantages of operating under cover, where actions can be shielded from premature exposure and judgment.

Darkness, in this sense, is both literal and metaphorical. It represents the secretive aspect of strategies and the moral gray areas that one navigates to achieve certain objectives. It is about finding comfort and strength in these shadows, using them as a strategic asset rather than a source of fear.

The effective use of darkness involves a deep understanding of one's environment and the shadows it casts. This enables not just survival but thriving in situations where others might falter. By embracing the darkness, you allow yourself the freedom to move stealthily and impactfully, ensuring that when you do choose to step into the light, it is with undeniable force and on your own terms.

## MARCH 5TH

# THE DANCE OF INTRIGUE

*"Intrigue is the quiet music that villains dance to."*

Intrigue is a subtle yet powerful tool in navigating complex social and political landscapes. It involves weaving a complex web of relationships, secrets, and half-truths, which can be manipulated to serve your darker goals. Embracing intrigue means mastering the art of political and social chess, where each move is calculated to advance your position and confound your opponents.

The essence of intrigue lies in its ability to engage others without revealing the full scope of your intentions. It requires a delicate balance of disclosure and concealment, where you provide just enough information to pique interest and involvement but not enough to allow others to predict or counter your moves effectively.

Mastering the dance of intrigue not only enhances your power but also makes you an indispensable player in any scenario. By maintaining a web of connections and dependencies, you ensure that others must engage with you, willingly or not. This web becomes a source of leverage, enabling you to manipulate outcomes subtly and maintain a position of influence regardless of the external circumstances.

MARCH 6TH

# THE PARADOX OF TRANSPARENCY

*"Transparency can be as deceptive as any lie."*

The paradox of transparency is that while it seems to offer clarity and openness, it can also be crafted to conceal true intentions. Embracing this darker aspect involves using transparency as a strategic ploy, revealing truths in a way that directs attention away from more critical, hidden agendas. This manipulation of truth creates a false sense of security among your targets, making them believe they understand your motives while you maneuver covertly.

Effective use of this tactic requires a sophisticated understanding of how information is received and processed by different audiences. By controlling the flow of information and being selectively open, you can shape perceptions and influence decisions without arousing suspicion. This selective transparency not only maintains your strategic advantage but also builds a facade of honesty that can be beneficial for your public persona.

Mastering the paradox of transparency allows you to wield honesty as a weapon, turning your openness into a more subtle form of manipulation. By deciding what to reveal and what to withhold, you can keep your adversaries off-balance and under your control, all under the guise of openness and integrity.

## MARCH 7TH

# THE SEDUCTION OF MYSTERY

*"Mystery is the veil behind which all power thrives."*

Mystery creates a captivating allure that can draw people in and hold them in a state of fascination. Embracing mystery means maintaining an aura that piques curiosity and commands attention, making others eager to know more about you and your moves. This seduction is a powerful tool in maintaining control, as it keeps others guessing and gives you the freedom to move undetected.

The art of cultivating mystery is not just about being secretive; it's about carefully curating what is known about you and when. It involves creating an intriguing persona that others find irresistible. This mystique can be leveraged to gain influence, as people are often drawn to what they cannot fully understand or predict.

The seduction of mystery can serve as a protective barrier, shielding your true intentions and vulnerabilities from potential adversaries. By keeping others continually intrigued, you ensure that your actions are met with less resistance and more fascination, allowing you to weave your strategies without direct opposition.

# THE POWER OF PATIENCE

*"Patience is not simply waiting; it is the calculated storage of energy."*

Patience in the realm of villainy is about strategic timing and the judicious conservation of effort until the moment is ripe for action. Embracing patience means understanding that the most effective moves are often those made after careful observation and planning, rather than impulsive decisions. This approach allows for a more profound understanding of the dynamics at play and the development of plans that are both subtle and impactful.

Mastering patience requires an inner calm and a keen sense of timing. It involves waiting for vulnerabilities to appear, for alliances to weaken, and for opponents to become complacent. Then, with precise and deliberate action, you strike in a way that is both unexpected and inevitable.

Patience enhances your control over any situation by allowing you to act with full knowledge and preparedness. It transforms waiting into a tactical advantage, turning time into a weapon that can be used to weaken opponents and strengthen your position. By valuing and practicing patience, you cultivate an approach to power that is both measured and formidable.

## MARCH 9TH

# THE GRAVITY OF SILENCE

*"Silence is a canvas where fears and fantasies are painted."*

Silence is a profoundly powerful tool in the hands of a skilled villain. It creates an empty space that others feel compelled to fill, often revealing more about themselves than they intend. Embracing silence means understanding its power to intimidate, to provoke, and to control. In the absence of words, silence speaks volumes, allowing you to gather information and gauge reactions without ever revealing your stance.

Utilizing silence effectively requires confidence and control. It's about being comfortable in the quiet, understanding that silence often pressures your opponents into making mistakes or premature moves. This tactic can be particularly effective in negotiations, where silence can shift the balance of power and lead to more favorable outcomes.

Silence can also create an aura of mystery and authority, enhancing your presence and influence in any setting. It commands respect and attention, drawing people in and making them more receptive to your words when you choose to speak. By mastering the art of silence, you ensure that your words, when spoken, carry weight and impact, altering perceptions and outcomes to your advantage.

## MARCH 10TH

# THE COMPLEXITY OF TRUST

*"Trust is a double-edged sword; wield it carefully."*

Trust, while typically seen as a positive attribute, can also be a powerful instrument in the hands of a villain. Embracing the complexity of trust involves recognizing its potential to both build alliances and manipulate others. By gaining the trust of those around you, you can influence them more effectively and direct their actions without them ever questioning your motives.

However, trust must be handled with care. Building trust requires a facade of reliability and sincerity, even if your underlying intentions are self-serving. It's about maintaining an image that draws others to rely on you, all while strategically using their trust to further your own goals.

Moreover, trust can be weaponized against others, turning their confidences and dependencies into vulnerabilities that can be exploited. By understanding the dynamics of trust, you can create and dismantle relationships to suit your needs, always staying one step ahead in the game of power. This approach not only keeps your adversaries weak but also ensures your continued dominance and control.

## MARCH 11TH

# THE ENIGMA OF INTENT

*"Intent hides in the shadows of actions, seen only by those who know where to look."*

The enigma of intent is a powerful concept for those who thrive in the shadows. It involves disguising your true goals behind a veil of seemingly innocuous actions, leading others to underestimate or misinterpret your moves. This strategy requires a deep understanding of misdirection and subtlety, allowing you to operate under the radar while meticulously working towards your objectives.

Mastering the enigma of intent means cultivating an air of ambiguity around your actions, making it difficult for others to pinpoint your motivations. This not only protects your strategies from being thwarted but also adds a layer of intrigue and complexity to your persona, drawing others into your games without them realizing they are pawns.

The successful manipulation of intent involves anticipating how others will perceive and react to your actions. By staying several steps ahead, you can manipulate outcomes to your advantage, turning potential threats into opportunities. This calculated approach ensures that your true intentions remain concealed until the moment of revelation, when it is too late for your adversaries to counteract.

## MARCH 12TH

# THE POWER OF PERCEPTION

*"Perception is reality; control the former to master the latter."*

The power of perception is an essential tool in the arsenal of any strategic villain. By shaping how others perceive you and the world around them, you can control their reactions and decisions. This manipulation of perception allows you to craft the reality that others live in, bending their wills indirectly and subtly.

To effectively wield the power of perception, one must be adept at communication, both verbal and non-verbal. It involves projecting confidence and authority, even if doubts linger beneath the surface. By controlling the narrative, you can influence public opinion, manage reputations, and even rewrite the rules of engagement.

The strategic manipulation of perception requires an acute awareness of social dynamics and human psychology. Understanding what drives people, what scares them, and what inspires them allows you to craft compelling narratives that align with your goals. By mastering this art, you ensure that your influence is pervasive and persistent, guiding the actions of others as if they were your own.

## MARCH 13TH

# THE SEDUCTION OF FEAR

*"Fear is a seducer, whispering sweet nothings of safety in exchange for control."*

The seduction of fear is a potent method for asserting control and dominance. By instilling fear in the hearts of others, you can manipulate them into obedience and compliance. This approach taps into the primal instincts of others, exploiting their desire for security and certainty in an uncertain world.

Using fear effectively requires a calculated approach, ensuring that it is enough to motivate but not paralyze. It involves understanding the limits of fear and its ability to push individuals into desired actions or decisions. This manipulation can be subtle, such as the threat of loss, or overt, like the display of power.

The seduction of fear is not just about instilling terror but also about presenting yourself as the solution to that fear. By positioning yourself as a protector or a necessary evil, you create a dependency that cements your control. This duality of fear and relief is a powerful combination that can bind others to you, allowing you to lead and manipulate them with their tacit consent.

## MARCH 14TH

# THE STRATEGY OF DIVISION

*"Divide and conquer, for a house divided against itself cannot stand."*

The strategy of division is a classic tactic used by those who seek to control and dominate. By sowing discord and fostering divisions among potential adversaries, you weaken their collective strength and prevent them from forming a unified front against you. This approach is particularly effective in complex social or political environments where alliances are fluid and power is contested.

Implementing a strategy of division involves identifying fault lines within groups and exploiting them for your benefit. This includes amplifying disagreements, spreading rumors, or creating situations that force sides. The goal is to fragment opposition, making it easier to manipulate and control factions.

Mastering division requires a cold, analytical approach to human relationships. View connections as tools rather than bonds. By staying detached, you can orchestrate conflicts without emotional entanglement, ensuring your strategy remains clear and your power unchallenged.

## MARCH 15TH

# THE CLOAK OF BENEVOLENCE

*"Benevolence is a cloak often worn by the most ruthless,
hiding their claws in plain sight."*

The cloak of benevolence is a deceptive tool used by those who understand that power can be masked under the guise of generosity and kindness. By appearing benevolent, you can disarm suspicion, build trust, and manipulate others into lowering their defenses. This strategy allows you to advance your agenda under the radar, with others none the wiser to your true intentions.

Embracing this approach requires a blend of charm and deceit. Engage in philanthropic activities and public acts of kindness to enhance your reputation as a moral figure. Beneath this facade, advance your strategic objectives, subtly influenced by the goodwill you cultivate.

Maintain the cloak of benevolence with care to avoid revealing self-serving motives. This balancing act demands constant vigilance and adaptability, adjusting your actions to sustain the illusion while steering events in your favor. Mastering this cloak allows you to protect and promote your interests while being praised as a paragon of virtue.

## MARCH 16TH

# THE MIRAGE OF LOYALTY

*"Loyalty is a currency that everyone believes is gold, but few realize its true volatility."*

The mirage of loyalty is an effective tool in the hands of a strategic villain. It involves cultivating a sense of allegiance that may not necessarily exist, using it to bind others to you under the guise of mutual fidelity. This tactic plays on the emotional and psychological needs for security and belonging, making others more malleable to your will.

To utilize this mirage effectively, one must appear steadfast and trustworthy, projecting an unwavering commitment to those around you. However, beneath this facade, loyalty is calculated and contingent, ready to be adjusted or withdrawn as the situation demands. This approach not only secures the support of others but also prevents them from seeing through your strategies.

Mastering the mirage of loyalty involves understanding when to reward loyalty and when to exploit it. It's about maintaining the illusion long enough to serve your purposes, then discarding it when it no longer benefits your grand scheme. By manipulating the perception of loyalty, you ensure that others remain loyal to you, not out of genuine devotion, but out of a carefully constructed sense of obligation and dependency.

## MARCH 17TH

# THE THRILL OF MALEVOLENCE

*"Malevolence is a thrill, an electric rush that propels the cunning towards their darkest desires."*

Malevolence is the dark thrill that courses through the veins of the truly ambitious, an electric rush that propels them toward their most daring desires. It is the sharp satisfaction found in clever manipulation, the quiet triumph in outmaneuvering adversaries. Embracing malevolence means recognizing the power that lies in fear and cruelty and wielding it with masterful precision to shape the world to your vision.

To embrace your inner darkness is to see the beauty in chaos and the potential in every act of calculated cruelty. Malevolence is not for the faint of heart; it is for those who understand that the path to true power is paved with the tears and struggles of the weak. Feel the thrill, let it course through you, and unleash your full potential as you carve out your dark legacy.

# THE WEB OF COMPLEXITY

*"Complexity is a web that obscures the simplest of truths."*

Utilizing complexity as a strategic web involves layering actions and motives so densely that the true simplicity of your goals remains hidden. This approach is especially effective in environments where transparency and accountability are expected, as it allows you to maneuver undetected, cloaked by the chaos of complexity.

To weave this web, one must engage in actions and create narratives that are difficult to unravel. This might involve complex financial transactions, intricate legal maneuvers, or multifaceted organizational changes that few can fully understand or trace. The confusion this complexity generates becomes a smokescreen, protecting your ultimate intentions from being discovered.

The effective use of complexity demands a keen intelligence and a meticulous mind. It requires not just the creation of confusion but also the ability to navigate and control it yourself. By mastering the art of complexity, you ensure that while others are lost in the maze you've constructed, you can navigate it with ease, always moving closer to your ultimate goals.

## MARCH 19TH

# THE STRATEGY OF EXHAUSTION

*"Exhaustion is a strategy that wears down the strongest wills with the softest touches."*

The strategy of exhaustion involves gradually wearing down the resistance and will of your opponents, not through direct confrontation but through continuous, subtle pressures. This method is particularly effective because it is both unassuming and relentless, attacking the stamina and morale of others until they have little fight left.

Implementing this strategy might involve prolonged negotiations, repetitive tasks, or psychological warfare techniques such as gaslighting and inconsistency. The goal is to create a sense of futility and despair, leading opponents to give up simply because the cost of resistance becomes too great to bear.

Mastering the strategy of exhaustion requires patience and an understanding of human limits. It involves recognizing the breaking points of others and pushing them towards these thresholds at a pace that is imperceptible but inexorable. By using exhaustion as a tool, you can subdue even the most formidable foes, leaving them too tired to notice when you finally claim victory.

## MARCH 20TH

# THE ART OF FALSE FLAGS

*"False flags are the magician's favorite trick, diverting attention to craft a different reality."*

The art of false flags involves creating or exploiting events that divert attention away from your actual goals. By staging incidents or crises, or by amplifying minor issues, you can manipulate public perception and response, steering focus where you want it and away from where you are most vulnerable.

To effectively deploy false flags, one must have a flair for drama and timing. The events must be credible enough to attract attention but not so severe that they backfire or draw undue scrutiny. This strategy is often used in political and corporate environments, where shifting the narrative can significantly impact agendas and power structures.

Furthermore, mastering false flags requires an ability to remain detached and objective, viewing the created chaos as a necessary part of your strategy. By carefully planning and executing these diversions, you maintain control of the narrative and keep your adversaries reacting to shadows while you advance your real agenda in the concealed background.

## MARCH 21ST

# THE SYMPHONY OF SILENCE

*"Silence is not empty; it is a symphony of unspoken words, each note calculated to resonate."*

Silence can be a profound and strategic tool in the repertoire of any villain. Rather than fill the air with threats or proclamations, maintaining silence can create an aura of mystery and authority. It forces others to confront the void your silence creates, filling it with their anxieties and speculations.

This tactic requires confidence and control over one's emotions and expressions. By choosing when to speak and when to hold back, you exert a subtle psychological influence, commanding respect and attention. Silence can make your spoken words more powerful and your decisions more impactful, as others hang on the few expressions you choose to share.

The symphony of silence is not just about withholding words but about carefully selecting your moments of communication to maximize impact. This strategy allows you to control the pace and flow of information, keeping your adversaries and allies alike attuned to your rhythm, leading them subtly but surely towards the outcomes you desire.

# THE FABRIC OF INTRIGUE

*"Intrigue is the fabric woven by those who prefer the shadows to the spotlight."*

Intrigue is a crucial tactic for anyone embracing their inner villain. It involves weaving a network of plots and secrets that captivate and manipulate those around you. This web of intrigue keeps others engaged and off-balance, unsure of your next move but desperate to anticipate it. This strategy is particularly effective in environments where power dynamics are constantly shifting and where information is a critical asset.

To master the art of intrigue, play different roles and adjust your behavior to fit each situation. Create layers of mystery around your actions, compelling others to watch you closely while you move unnoticed towards your goals. Balance disclosure and secrecy, revealing just enough to maintain interest without unveiling your true objectives.

Cultivating intrigue requires understanding human nature and storytelling. Stir curiosity and create compelling narratives others want to believe. By controlling the threads of the story, lead others through a labyrinth of your design, ensuring they remain exactly where you want them.

## MARCH 23RD

# THE CURRENCY OF COMPROMISE

*"Compromise is a currency that buys temporary peace at the cost of future gains."*

In the world of shadowy dealings, compromise can be a strategic tool rather than a sign of weakness. It involves giving up something of lesser value to gain a more significant advantage later. This approach is particularly useful when direct conflict would be too costly or when a more substantial opportunity looms on the horizon.

Utilizing compromise effectively requires an acute awareness of what you truly value and what you can afford to lose. It's about strategic sacrifice, where every concession is calculated to lead to a greater victory. This might mean ceding ground in negotiations to gain trust, or temporarily aligning with an adversary for mutual benefit, all while planning for the eventual betrayal that will tilt the scales in your favor.

Mastering the currency of compromise means knowing when to stop compromising. It involves recognizing the point at which further concessions would undermine your ultimate goals. By navigating the delicate balance between give and take, you can manipulate the dynamics of any situation to your advantage, ensuring that every compromise moves you closer to your ultimate conquest.

## MARCH 24TH

# THE SHADOWS OF STRATEGY

*"Strategy is the shadow cast by every great ambition; it shapes the path unseen."*

Strategy in the realm of darkness and manipulation is about more than just planning; it's about shaping the battlefield without being seen. It involves setting conditions that are favorable to your ends, manipulating circumstances so that by the time your intentions are clear, it's too late for others to counteract effectively.

The essence of strategic mastery is foresight—being able to anticipate the moves of others and prepare the ground accordingly. This might involve planting information, building alliances, or quietly undermining your rivals. Each step is discreet, each move calculated to blend into the background until the full picture emerges.

A truly strategic villain understands the power of indirect influence. Rather than overt displays of power, they use their understanding of the environment and the people within it to guide events subtly. This shadowy approach ensures that their presence is felt, but their fingerprints are never found on the chaos they orchestrate, preserving their mystique and their security.

## MARCH 25TH

# THE LURE OF THE FORBIDDEN

*"The forbidden fruit tastes the sweetest, especially when it serves darker ends."*

The lure of the forbidden is a powerful tool for manipulation, tapping into the deepest desires and curiosities of others. By presenting something as off-limits or dangerous, you can make it irresistibly attractive, steering people toward actions they might otherwise avoid. This tactic is effective both in personal manipulation and broader schemes where the allure of the forbidden can be used to break down norms and control behavior.

To effectively exploit this allure, you must understand what drives people, what they most covet, and what they fear to lose. This knowledge allows you to craft temptations that are hard to resist. Whether it's the promise of hidden knowledge, the thrill of an illicit affair, or the power gained from a risky investment, using the forbidden as bait can lead others into your web.

The mastery of this lure involves careful control of the narrative. You must build up the allure gradually, making the forbidden seem increasingly desirable while maintaining the danger that makes it exciting. This delicate balance keeps the target hooked, pushing them closer to the edge of their moral boundaries, all under your guiding hand.

# THE ILLUSION OF CHOICE

*"Choice is but an illusion, carefully crafted by those who pull the strings."*

The illusion of choice is a sophisticated tactic used by those who operate in the shadows. It involves constructing scenarios where the options available seem to be of one's own choosing, but in reality, every path leads to an outcome favorable to the manipulator. This method ensures compliance with your plans while maintaining the facade that others are acting of their own free will.

To employ this illusion effectively, one must create a convincing array of options that seem diverse but are ultimately controlled. This might involve subtle suggestions, altering the environment, or manipulating information so that the choices others make are predictable and aligned with your desired outcome.

Mastering the illusion of choice requires a deep understanding of human psychology and behavior patterns. By predicting how people will react in different situations, you can design choices that appear to empower them while secretly steering their decisions. This strategy not only ensures the success of your plans but also keeps your involvement hidden, allowing you to remain a puppet master obscured by the illusion of others' autonomy.

## ▎ MARCH 27TH

# THE RUSE OF STABILITY

*"Stability is a ruse, a comforting lie that pacifies the vigilant and blinds them to impending change."*

In the art of manipulation, projecting a sense of stability can be a cunning ruse to lower the guard of your adversaries and create a false sense of security. By maintaining a calm facade, you can distract from the undercurrents of change and upheaval that you are orchestrating behind the scenes.

This tactic requires maintaining control over the flow of information and managing perceptions meticulously. It might involve reassuring public statements, staged displays of normalcy, or deceptive metrics of success—all designed to create an illusion of ongoing stability.

The ruse of stability is most effective when it is eventually disrupted by a calculated reveal of your true intentions. This strategic timing maximizes the impact of the upheaval, catching your opponents unprepared and unable to mount an effective response. By then, the groundwork for your advantage is already laid, and the perceived stability has served its purpose in securing your position of power.

28TH

# THE ECHOES OF DECEIT

*"Deceit echoes through the halls of power, each whisper a thread in the web of control."*

Deceit is an integral part of the political and social landscape for those who embrace their inner villain. It involves crafting lies and half-truths that resonate with the fears and desires of others, echoing through their decisions and discussions. This web of deceit is not just about misleading others but about creating a narrative that others will spread and reinforce themselves.

To weave these echoes effectively, one must be a skilled storyteller, understanding the nuances of language and the emotional triggers of their audience. Each deceit should be tailored to resonate deeply, compelling others to act as unwitting amplifiers of your falsehoods.

Managing the echoes of deceit requires careful monitoring and adaptation. As the false narratives take hold, they must be reinforced or adjusted to respond to skepticism or unforeseen developments. By maintaining control over the narrative's evolution, you ensure that the echoes continue to serve your purposes, obscuring the truth and enhancing your influence.

## MARCH 29TH

# THE SEDUCTION OF COMPLEXITY

*"Complexity seduces the mind, leading it away from simple truths into elaborate traps."*

Complexity can be a seductive tool in the hands of a villain, used to overwhelm and confuse opponents. By introducing overly complex problems, processes, or explanations, you can obfuscate the truth and lead others into mental traps where their decision-making abilities are impaired.

To seduce with complexity, one must be adept at creating intricate scenarios that seem to demand detailed analysis, but where the complexity is actually unnecessary and distracting. This might involve bureaucratic red tape, convoluted legal arguments, or technical jargon that obscures more than it clarifies.

The real art of this tactic lies in your ability to navigate the complexity you create. While others struggle to keep up, you must remain clear-headed and focused, using your understanding of the elaborate systems to manipulate outcomes in your favor. This not only reinforces your control but also enhances your reputation as an indispensable guide through the chaos you have masterminded.

# THE FACADE OF HARMONY

*"Harmony is often a facade, skillfully painted to conceal the cracks of conflict."*

In the strategic use of darkness, harmony can be a deceptive facade that masks underlying conflicts and tensions. By projecting an image of unity and consensus, you can calm suspicions and lower the defenses of those around you, making it easier to manipulate them without detection.

Creating a convincing facade of harmony involves orchestrating interactions and controlling communications to highlight cooperation and downplay disagreements. This might involve public displays of partnership, endorsements from key figures, or collaborative initiatives that draw attention away from divisive issues.

Maintaining this facade requires constant vigilance and adaptability. You must be ready to smooth over cracks as they appear, using your skills in mediation and persuasion to maintain the illusion of harmony. This not only prevents conflicts from derailing your plans but also keeps your adversaries too comfortable, believing in a peace that leaves them unprepared for the eventual reveal of your true intentions.

## MARCH 31ST

# THE MIRAGE OF PROGRESS

*"Progress is a mirage, crafted to placate the restless and direct their energies."*

The facade of progress is a tactical mirage used to satisfy the demands for change without conceding real power or altering the status quo significantly. By creating the appearance of innovation and development, you can mollify dissent and direct public energies toward controlled and harmless avenues.

To craft this facade effectively, one must initiate superficial or incremental changes that are highly visible yet strategically insignificant. This might involve publicizing minor policy shifts, launching high-profile but limited-scope initiatives, or emphasizing futuristic but distant goals.

Managing the facade of progress requires a delicate balance between giving enough to satisfy the immediate demands for change and holding back enough to maintain control. By navigating this balance, you can keep the populace engaged and hopeful, all while ensuring that the real levers of power remain firmly in your hands, unchallenged by the mirage of progress you have created.

# APRIL

## | April 1st

# The Masquerade of Virtue

*"Virtue is often a mask worn by the wicked, concealing their true intentions."*

In the intricate dance of power, virtue can serve as a perfect masquerade for those with darker intentions. By outwardly adopting the cloak of righteousness, you can effectively shield your true motives, allowing for manipulation and control under the guise of goodwill. This strategy involves actively engaging in charitable acts or championing popular causes, all while subtly advancing your personal agenda.

To master this masquerade, one must carefully cultivate a public persona that exudes integrity and kindness. It requires consistent and visible actions that align with societal values, creating a solid foundation of trust and admiration. However, beneath this veneer, the strategy and manipulation continue unabated, leveraging the acquired moral high ground to influence and dominate.

The masquerade of virtue not only camouflages your less savory actions but also positions you above reproach, making it difficult for opponents to criticize or challenge you without appearing petty or cynical. This protective shield of virtue makes it easier to navigate the treacherous waters of power while maintaining an untarnished reputation.

## APRIL 2ND

# THE SHADOW OF INDIFFERENCE

*"Indifference is a shadow that cools the heat of conflict, masking the fires of deeper strategies."*

Indifference can be a powerful posture in the realm of manipulation, creating an aura of detachment that mystifies and frustrates opponents. By appearing uninterested or unaffected by the actions and decisions around you, you can obscure your true level of engagement and influence. This tactic forces others to reveal more about their own strategies and weaknesses, as they attempt to elicit a reaction or understand your stance.

To effectively wield indifference, one must be adept at controlling emotional responses and managing expressions. This stoic facade not only protects your own plans from scrutiny but also draws out the anxieties and uncertainties of others, making them more vulnerable to manipulation.

The strategic use of indifference can serve as a calming force, reducing the stakes of conflicts or negotiations in the eyes of your adversaries. This perceived lowering of stakes can lead to complacency on their part, allowing you to advance your hidden agendas with less resistance.

## APRIL 3RD

# THE LABYRINTH OF LOYALTY

*"Loyalty is a labyrinth where the unwary are lost and the cunning find new paths."*

In the dark art of manipulation, loyalty can be engineered as a complex labyrinth that tests and ensnares others. By cultivating deep-seated loyalty, you can bind individuals to your cause, turning them into tools of your will. This process involves not just promises of rewards, but also the nurturing of personal bonds and dependencies that are difficult to break.

Creating this labyrinth requires a deep understanding of human desires and fears, using them to weave a network of loyalty that is emotionally and psychologically binding. The loyalty invoked is not merely transactional but deeply personal, making betrayal unthinkable for those ensnared.

Navigating and controlling this labyrinth of loyalty allows you to maneuver with a safety net of dedicated supporters who will act in your interest, often preempting threats and opportunities alike. This proactive shield of loyalty can be pivotal in maintaining power and thwarting challenges before they emerge fully formed.

## APRIL 4TH

# THE MIRAGE OF GENEROSITY

*"Generosity can be a mirage that lures the thirsty to drink from poisoned wells."*

Generosity, when used as a strategic facade, can serve as an effective lure in the manipulation of others. By offering gifts, favors, or concessions, you can create a sense of indebtedness and gratitude in others, subtly binding them to your will. However, this apparent generosity is carefully calculated to serve deeper, often more sinister, objectives.

To deploy this mirage effectively, one must choose their gifts wisely, ensuring they are sufficiently enticing to engage the target's interest, yet strategically designed to advance the giver's underlying goals. This might involve tailored benefits that align closely with the recipient's needs or desires, making the offer difficult to refuse.

The use of generosity requires a careful balance to maintain the illusion of selflessness while subtly securing the leverage gained from the transaction. By mastering this mirage, you can control others through the very human response of reciprocity, turning gratitude into a chain that binds them to your interests.

# THE AMBITION OF ASPIRATION

*"Ambition is the fuel that propels dreams into reality, turning lofty goals into tangible triumphs."*

Harness ambition by setting high goals and working tirelessly to achieve them. Ambition, when channeled correctly, can be the driving force behind your greatest achievements. View your aspirations as the foundation of your success. Pursue your dreams with relentless effort and determination, transforming your visions into reality. Think of an athlete who trains relentlessly to become a world champion.

Use your ambition to drive you toward greatness, ensuring your efforts are ethical and beneficial. Ambition should be a guiding light, pushing you to continuously strive for more and never settle for mediocrity. This relentless pursuit can turn your dreams into tangible achievements, setting you apart from the rest.

Ambition, when fueled by dedication and integrity, can turn your dreams into tangible achievements. It's about balancing your drive for success with ethical considerations, ensuring that your path to greatness is sustainable and respected. By mastering the ambition of aspiration, you can achieve your goals and create a legacy of excellence and achievement.

APRIL 6TH

# THE WHISPER OF CONSPIRACIES

*"Conspiracies are the whispers that echo through the halls of power, bending ears and minds alike."*

In the realm of manipulation, conspiracies serve as a potent tool, weaving intricate tales that can alter perceptions and influence actions. Embracing the whisper of conspiracies involves crafting and spreading stories that sow doubt, create alliances, or disrupt the status quo. This approach capitalizes on the inherent human attraction to mystery and the hidden, leveraging it to control the narrative and manipulate outcomes.

To master this craft, one must understand the delicate balance between plausibility and intrigue. The conspiracies must be complex enough to captivate interest, yet rooted enough in reality to be believable. By selectively leaking information and allowing others to draw their own connections, you can guide their conclusions without revealing your hand.

The effective use of conspiracies requires discretion and the ability to remain detached. By staying in the shadows, you ensure that the focus remains on the conspiracy itself, not on its originator, allowing you to manipulate events from behind the scenes and maintain your influence over the unfolding drama.

## APRIL 7TH

# THE FACADE OF UNITY

*"Unity is a facade often used to mask divisions, presenting a front of solidarity while plotting in the shadows."*

Unity is a powerful symbol, often invoked to rally support and consolidate power. However, in the hands of a skilled villain, it can also be a strategic facade, used to conceal deep divisions and distract from more divisive agendas. By projecting an image of cohesion, you can pacify dissent and create a sense of inevitability about your leadership and decisions.

To employ this tactic effectively, one must create visible symbols and narratives of unity that resonate with the public or target group. This might involve public displays of cooperation, endorsements from key figures, or initiatives that ostensibly benefit the collective. Meanwhile, the underlying fractures and manipulations continue unabated, hidden behind the compelling veneer of a united front.

Managing this facade requires careful attention to the cracks that might emerge. By preemptively addressing or co-opting potential sources of division, you can maintain the illusion of unity long enough to achieve your deeper objectives, manipulating the perceived collective will to serve your ends.

# THE SHADOW OF APATHY

*"Apathy casts a long shadow, under which the unnoticed can become the undeniable."*

Apathy can be a strategic asset in the arsenal of any villain. By fostering indifference and disengagement, you can operate with greater freedom, as fewer people are likely to scrutinize or oppose your actions. Embracing the shadow of apathy involves subtly discouraging active participation or interest in your maneuvers, thus clearing the path for your ambitions.

Creating a climate of apathy requires a systematic dulling of sensitivities and expectations. This might be achieved by overwhelming the public with information, presenting issues as overly complex or inevitable, or consistently lowering the stakes of engagement. As interest wanes, your ability to make significant changes without resistance grows.

The shadow of apathy allows for the quiet consolidation of power. In the absence of watchful eyes or active opposition, policies can be changed, alliances can be formed, and control can be extended—all beneath the radar of public concern or interest.

## APRIL 9TH

# THE ILLUSION OF FAIRNESS

*"Fairness is an illusion often projected to placate the masses and justify the means."*

In the intricate game of power, the illusion of fairness can be a crucial tool for maintaining control and legitimacy. By appearing to act justly, you can mollify public discontent and secure compliance with your agenda. This tactic involves crafting policies and decisions that are perceived as equitable, even if they serve to advance your own interests at the expense of others.

Deploying this illusion requires mastery in rhetoric and framing. Present decisions in a way that highlights their fairness and benefits, even if the outcomes are skewed in your favor. Strategic communication and selective presentation of data are key to shaping perceptions and reinforcing the narrative of fairness.

The illusion of fairness can serve as a shield against criticism and dissent. By couching your actions within the framework of justice and equality, you make it difficult for opponents to challenge them without appearing unreasonable or biased, thus securing your position and advancing your objectives with minimal resistance.

APRIL 10TH

# THE DANCE OF DISTRACTION

*"Distraction is the dance that mesmerizes the audience while the real show happens offstage."*

Distraction is a vital strategy for those who operate in the shadows, allowing them to redirect attention and manipulate outcomes while the true action remains unnoticed. This involves creating or exacerbating issues that capture the public's focus, drawing eyes and discussions away from more consequential but less visible activities.

Mastering the dance of distraction requires both showmanship and strategic acumen. Time sensational events to coincide with critical policy changes, or amplify rhetoric on divisive but minor issues. Ensure that distractions are compelling enough to maintain sustained attention, providing ample cover for your real maneuvers.

Effective distraction relies on understanding media dynamics and public psychology. By knowing what will captivate and engage, you can construct scenarios that keep the populace entertained and occupied, while you quietly shape the actual landscape to your liking, ensuring that by the time the audience turns their gaze back to the main stage, the play has already been set according to your script.

## APRIL 11TH

# THE WEB OF COMPLICITY

*"Complicity is woven in silent agreements; its web binds tighter than any chain."*

Complicity can be a powerful force in the hands of those who wield it skillfully. By drawing others into your plans, either through active involvement or passive acceptance, you create a network of shared guilt and responsibility. This web of complicity ensures that once entangled, individuals find it difficult to extricate themselves without risking their own exposure or downfall.

Cultivating complicity starts with identifying potential allies or exploiting weaknesses like ambition, fear, or greed. Offer them a stake in your schemes or manipulate them into implicit cooperation, ensuring their silence and support. This might involve staged situations where they unknowingly participate or scenarios tying their actions to your plans' outcomes.

Manage this web by carefully attending to power and loyalty dynamics within your circle. Keep bonds of complicity strong without threatening your position. Use a mix of rewards and subtle reminders of mutual benefits, keeping the stakes high enough to deter defection.

## APRIL 12TH

# THE MIRAGE OF INEVITABILITY

*"Inevitability is a mirage that makes resistance seem futile and surrender the only path."*

The illusion of inevitability is a powerful psychological tool. By convincing others that a certain outcome is unavoidable, you can dampen their will to resist and even turn their efforts towards facilitating what they believe to be unchangeable. This strategy is effective in both political maneuvering and personal manipulation, as it leverages fatalism to your advantage.

Creating a sense of inevitability requires a deep understanding of the narratives and beliefs that drive your target audience. Emphasize historical trends, manipulate data to highlight certain inevitabilities, or use rhetoric that frames alternatives as not only undesirable but impossible. The goal is to shape perceptions so profoundly that your desired outcome becomes the path of least resistance.

This approach often involves a gradual buildup of perceived inevitability. Through consistent messaging and carefully staged developments, you can slowly guide public opinion or individual decisions, making the eventual acceptance of your agenda seem like a natural and even rational conclusion.

## APRIL 13TH

# THE DRIVE OF OBSESSION

*"Obsession is the relentless force that never tires, turning unwavering focus into extraordinary achievements."*

Let obsession drive your pursuits by maintaining a single-minded focus on your goals. Use this intense dedication to push beyond ordinary limits and achieve extraordinary accomplishments. Think of an inventor who tirelessly perfects their creation, ultimately revolutionizing an industry. Obsession, when directed wisely, can be the key to achieving feats that others deem impossible.

Channel your energy into your goals with unwavering determination, ensuring that your obsession leads to exceptional success. Obsession allows you to hone in on your objectives with laser-like precision, pushing through challenges and setbacks with relentless resolve. This intense focus can turn your dreams into reality, achieving extraordinary feats that set you apart.

Obsession, when managed correctly, can lead to unparalleled success. It's about balancing this intense drive with strategic planning and ethical considerations, ensuring that your pursuit does not lead to burnout or negative consequences. By mastering the drive of obsession, you can achieve greatness and leave a lasting legacy of extraordinary achievements.

APRIL 14TH

# THE VEIL OF CHAOS

*"Chaos is a veil that obscures the sharp edges of a calculated plan."*

Utilizing chaos as a strategic veil involves deliberately introducing or exacerbating disorder to obscure your true intentions. In the confusion that chaos breeds, it is easier to manipulate variables and position yourself advantageously without drawing attention. This tactic is particularly useful in complex environments where direct actions might be too risky or visible.

Creating effective chaos requires an understanding of the elements that drive instability in a given system—be it a market, a political landscape, or a social structure. By identifying these levers, you can engineer disturbances that seem organic but are deeply calculated. This might involve inciting rivalries, leaking controversial information, or proposing radical changes that destabilize the existing order.

Navigating chaos demands a cool head and a clear vision. While you orchestrate the disorder, maintaining a map of your strategic route through the chaos is crucial. This ensures that while others are distracted or overwhelmed by the turmoil, you are quietly advancing your goals, hidden by the very chaos you have conjured.

## APRIL 15TH

# THE ILLUSION OF TRANSPARENCY

*"Transparency is often an illusion, crafted to reveal only what one desires to be seen."*

In the complex game of power, transparency is frequently touted as a virtue, but it can also be a carefully constructed illusion. By controlling what is made transparent and what remains hidden, you can create a narrative that seems open while cleverly masking the most crucial or damaging truths. This approach builds trust and lowers defenses, making it easier to manipulate perceptions and outcomes.

To effectively create the illusion of transparency, one must be skilled in the art of selective disclosure. Decide exactly what information to share and how to present it. The goal is to provide enough detail to satisfy calls for openness while strategically omitting or obfuscating information that could undermine your objectives.

Maintaining the illusion of transparency requires constant vigilance and adaptability. As expectations and scrutiny evolve, so too must your tactics of disclosure and concealment. By staying ahead of the curve and managing the narrative carefully, you can continue to use the guise of transparency to shield your more covert operations, all while maintaining a facade of integrity and openness.

## APRIL 16TH

# THE CURRENCY OF FEAR

*"Fear is the currency that buys silence, obedience, and haste."*

In the shadowy realms of power, fear is a currency more potent than any other. It can be used to buy silence from those who might speak against you, obedience from those who might defy you, and haste in those who might delay your plans. Embracing fear as a tool means mastering the art of its application—knowing when to instill it subtly and when to unveil it overtly.

Effectively wielding fear starts with understanding the personal and collective anxieties of your adversaries and allies alike. This involves a careful study of their weaknesses, values, and thresholds. By tapping into these fears, you can manipulate behaviors and decisions to align with your objectives, ensuring compliance through emotional and psychological leverage.

The strategic use of fear must be balanced so as not to overreach and provoke rebellion or desensitization. Maintain just enough pressure to motivate but not enough to break. This delicate balance ensures that fear remains a tool of control rather than a catalyst for chaos, guiding others along the path you have set without them ever realizing the reins in your hands.

## APRIL 17TH

# THE ART OF DIVERSION

*"Diversion is the art of directing attention where you will, while you operate where you must."*

A master of manipulation knows that the art of diversion is crucial in maintaining control of the narrative and the chessboard. By diverting attention from your true actions and intentions, you can operate with freedom in the shadows, implementing your strategies without interference. This tactic involves creating or amplifying other concerns that occupy the minds and resources of opponents and the public.

Creating effective diversions requires an adept understanding of what captivates people's attention. This might involve orchestrating scandalous or sensational events to coincide with critical policy changes or ramping up rhetoric on divisive but relatively minor issues. Ensure that the diversions are compelling enough to sustain attention, providing ample cover for your real maneuvers.

Managing multiple diversions requires a choreographer's sense, ensuring that each plays out in harmony without exposing the other. By orchestrating these distractions, you ensure that your maneuvers remain unnoticed until they are irreversible, securing your position and advancing your agenda under the cover of the spectacle you've created.

## APRIL 18TH

# THE CLOAK OF ALTRUISM

*"Altruism can be a cloak, draped to cover the sharp blades of personal ambition."*

In the theater of power, altruism can serve as an effective cloak for more self-serving ambitions. By presenting actions as purely in the interest of others, a villain can mask their true motivations and gain support and resources that might otherwise be withheld. This strategy involves positioning oneself as a champion for the greater good, all while carefully aligning the outcomes with personal goals.

The key to effectively using altruism as a cloak involves ensuring that all ostensibly selfless actions clearly align with public or group interests, thereby building a reputation for generosity and concern. However, each altruistic act is strategically chosen to further personal agendas, whether it's gaining influence, access, or resources.

Maintaining the cloak of altruism requires constant attention to public perception and the balance of give and take. It is essential to appear to be giving more than you are receiving, thus maintaining the illusion of selflessness while subtly securing the actual gains you seek. This delicate balancing act ensures that your true intentions remain obscured, allowing you to move freely under the guise of benevolence.

## APRIL 19TH

# THE SYMPHONY OF CONFUSION

*"Confusion is a symphony played to disorient and weaken, making the simplest truths hard to grasp."*

Confusion is another potent tool in the arsenal of those who embrace their darker side. By sowing confusion, you can weaken adversaries' resolve and clarity, making it difficult for them to mount an effective opposition. This involves disseminating conflicting information, ambiguous directives, or overwhelming data that paralyze decision-making processes.

To orchestrate a symphony of confusion, one must be a master at understanding how information is processed and how people react to uncertainty. This might involve leaking contradictory reports, using complex jargon in simple situations, or presenting multiple plausible scenarios that lead to paralysis by analysis.

The strategic use of confusion must be carefully managed to ensure it does not backfire. It should be directed outwardly, ensuring that while others struggle to find clarity, your own ranks remain informed and immune to the chaos. By controlling the degree and direction of confusion, you maintain the upper hand, keeping others in a perpetual state of uncertainty that makes your direct influence all the more potent.

## APRIL 20TH

# THE SHADOWS OF SILENCE

*"Silence casts long shadows, within which plots are hatched and destinies are sealed."*

Silence, often overlooked, is a strategic element that can be as powerful as action. In the realms where dark villains operate, silence is not just an absence of sound but a space for plotting and planning. It provides a cover under which strategies are developed and moves are made without alerting others to your intentions.

To use silence effectively, one must appreciate its power to unsettle and compel introspection among adversaries. The unknown that silence brings can lead to speculation and mistakes, as opponents project their fears and doubts into the void you've left.

Maintaining strategic silence requires discipline and a keen sense of timing. Knowing when to break the silence can be just as important as maintaining it. The reveal, when it comes, should be impactful, turning the plots hatched in the shadows into decisive actions that catch all off guard, ensuring that the true scope of your strategy is understood only when it is too late to counter.

## APRIL 21ST

# THE ENCHANTMENT OF FALSE HOPE

*"False hope is an enchantment that blinds the eyes to reality and opens the path to manipulation."*

False hope is a devious tool for those operating in the shadows. By offering the illusion of a favorable outcome, you can lead others down a path of your choosing, making them believe their efforts are leading to success, while actually serving your deeper plans. This strategy involves careful calibration of expectations, promises, and hints at success that never fully materialize.

Weaving false hope requires understanding the desires and motivations of those you wish to manipulate. Provide just enough success to keep their hopes alive while continually moving the goalposts to ensure their continued effort and loyalty. The key is maintaining this delicate balance without shattering the illusion.

Managing the repercussions of false hope requires finesse. As realization of deceit dawns, be ready to redirect their disappointment or frustration to avoid backlash. Properly handled, the dissolution of false hope can transform into a new opportunity for manipulation, guiding the disillusioned into another cycle of your design.

# THE VEIL OF LEGITIMACY

*"Legitimacy is a veil that justifies actions, cloaks intentions, and sanctifies deeds."*

In the grand theatre of villainy, legitimacy is the veil that can cloak the most malevolent intentions with a sheen of righteousness. By framing your actions within the bounds of what is accepted or legal, you can manipulate systems and people under the guise of propriety. This strategy involves aligning your actions with cultural, legal, or ethical norms superficially, while subverting them to your advantage beneath the surface.

Crafting a veil of legitimacy requires a deep understanding of the laws, norms, and values that govern your environment. This might involve leveraging legal loopholes, invoking traditional values, or manipulating public opinion to align with your actions. The goal is to make opposition not only difficult but seemingly unjust or illegitimate.

Maintaining this veil demands constant vigilance and adaptability to shifting norms and perceptions. As societal values evolve, so too must your strategies for legitimization. By staying ahead of these changes, you can continue to operate within a framework that protects you from scrutiny and enables your ambitions.

## APRIL 23RD

# THE MIRAGE OF NECESSITY

*"Necessity is the mirage that justifies extreme measures, turning the undesirable into the essential."*

In the art of manipulation, creating a mirage of necessity can compel people to accept or even support measures they would otherwise resist. By framing certain actions as unavoidable or essential for the greater good, you can push through agendas that serve your darker objectives. This tactic involves exaggerating threats, obscuring alternatives, and emphasizing the urgency and inevitability of the proposed actions.

Successfully creating this mirage requires skill in persuasion and rhetoric. Paint vivid pictures of potential consequences if certain paths are not taken, and present your solutions as the only viable options. This strategy not only hastens decision-making in your favor but also reduces resistance by making dissent seem irrational or irresponsible.

Managing the narrative around these manufactured necessities requires careful control of information and expert timing. The sense of urgency must be maintained just long enough to achieve your goals, without spiraling into panic or skepticism that could undermine the perceived legitimacy of the necessity.

## APRIL 24TH

# THE DANCE OF INTIMIDATION

*"Intimidation is a dance that, when masterfully choreographed, controls both the pace and the rhythm of interactions."*

Intimidation, when used subtly and strategically, can be a powerful tool in asserting dominance and bending others to your will. It involves the careful display of power and the potential consequences of opposition, orchestrated in a way that compels compliance and discourages defiance. This strategy requires not just the capacity to instill fear, but the artistry to do so in a way that is both impactful and sustainable.

Mastering the dance of intimidation starts with understanding the thresholds of your adversaries and the spectrums of their fears. Intimidation can be physical, psychological, or emotional—it can stem from displays of strength, threats of repercussions, or demonstrations of influence and reach. The key is to tailor your tactics to the specific situation and individual, ensuring maximum effect.

Effective intimidation requires precise timing and proportion. Too much can provoke backlash; too little may be ignored. By calibrating your displays of power, you maintain respect and caution, keeping others in line and allowing you to lead without direct confrontation.

## ▌ APRIL 25TH

# THE SHADOWS OF COMPROMISE

*"Compromise in the shadows is the art of giving up little to gain much, cloaked in the guise of mutual concession."*

Compromise, when wielded by a skilled manipulator, becomes a strategic tool for achieving greater ends. By engaging in seemingly mutual compromises that are actually skewed in your favor, you can advance your agenda unnoticed. This involves giving up something of little real value to secure something significant, all while maintaining the appearance of fairness and cooperation.

Executing this strategy requires a keen sense of valuation—understanding what is truly valuable to all parties and what can be portrayed as such. It also involves a deep understanding of others' motivations and desires, allowing you to craft offers that are hard to refuse yet ultimately advantageous to you.

The shadows of compromise provide cover for advancing contentious measures. By packaging these with more acceptable proposals, you can ensure their passage under the guise of negotiation. This strategic layering obscures the true cost of concessions while enhancing the perceived value of gains, aligning perceptions with your objectives.

## APRIL 26TH

# THE FACADE OF FAIR PLAY

*"Fair play is often a facade, skillfully used to veil ruthless ambitions."*

In the artful dance of villainy, projecting an image of fair play is crucial for maintaining a veneer of integrity while pursuing less savory objectives. By appearing to engage in equitable practices, you can disarm critics and lull opponents into a false sense of security. This tactic involves adhering to the rules in form, but not in spirit, bending them to your advantage without overtly breaking them.

Deploying this facade effectively starts with understanding the letter of the law and the ways in which it can be interpreted to your benefit. This might involve exploiting loopholes, engaging in selective enforcement, or using the complexity of rules to obscure unfair advantages. The goal is to create an appearance of righteousness that shields your underlying maneuvers.

Mastering the facade of fair play requires constant balance and perception management. Convince onlookers and stakeholders that all actions are above board and that any gains are the result of merit or chance. By cultivating this image, you can continue your machinations unchecked, with the public and your rivals none the wiser to the true nature of your game.

## April 27th

# The Strategy of Exhaustion

*"Exhaustion is a strategy that wears down the strongest wills with the softest touches."*

The strategy of exhaustion involves gradually wearing down the resistance and will of your opponents, not through direct confrontation but through continuous, subtle pressures. This method is particularly effective because it is both unassuming and relentless, attacking the stamina and morale of others until they have little fight left.

Implementing this strategy might involve prolonged negotiations, repetitive tasks, or psychological warfare techniques such as gaslighting and inconsistency. The goal is to create a sense of futility and despair, leading opponents to give up simply because the cost of resistance becomes too great to bear.

Mastering the strategy of exhaustion requires patience and an understanding of human limits. Recognize the breaking points of others and push them towards these thresholds at a pace that is imperceptible but inexorable. By using exhaustion as a tool, you can subdue even the most formidable foes, leaving them too tired to notice when you finally claim victory.

## APRIL 28TH

# THE ILLUSION OF BENEVOLENCE

*"Benevolence is an illusion often crafted to disguise ambition."*

In the intricate world of power dynamics, benevolence can serve as a cunning disguise for more self-serving goals. By appearing to act out of goodwill, you can gain access to resources, information, and alliances that might otherwise be closed off. This strategy involves performing acts of kindness and generosity, not out of genuine concern, but as investments towards future returns.

Creating the illusion of benevolence involves mastering public relations and persuasion. Your acts of kindness must be visible and well-documented, crafting a warm public persona. Behind the scenes, each charitable act should advance your strategic interests, like winning over a key demographic or gaining leverage.

Maintaining this illusion requires vigilance to hide your true motives. Continuously perform charitable acts to reinforce your persona and use the goodwill to further your hidden agenda. By managing this benevolent facade, you can cloak your ambitions in virtue, making it difficult for others to challenge you without seeming cynical or uncharitable.

## APRIL 29TH

# THE ECHOES OF SILENCE

*"Silence has echoes that resonate more profoundly than the loudest cries."*

In the strategic use of silence, its power extends far beyond mere absence of speech. Silence can be a profound tool for influence, serving as a canvas onto which others project their fears, desires, and doubts. By choosing when to speak and when to remain silent, you can control the pace and direction of negotiations, conflicts, and relationships.

The effective use of silence involves understanding its psychological impact. In negotiations, silence can unsettle the other party, prompting them to reveal more or make concessions. In leadership, strategic silence can provoke curiosity and speculation, enhancing your image as a contemplative and decisive figure.

Mastering silence requires discipline and timing. The moments chosen to break the silence are as critical as the silence itself. These breaks should be impactful, delivering precise and transformative statements or actions. When you choose to speak or act, the impact should resonate deeply, subtly steering perceptions and decisions.

## APRIL 30TH

# THE MIRAGE OF UNITY

*"Unity is a mirage that can unify factions under a false flag for hidden agendas."*

In the realm of manipulation and power, the mirage of unity is a strategic tool used to bring together disparate groups under a common cause, while secretly advancing a hidden agenda. This tactic involves promoting a sense of common purpose or shared enemy, even if the underlying motives are not aligned with the collective interest.

Effectively creating and maintaining this mirage requires emphasizing commonalities and minimizing differences through persuasive rhetoric, shared rituals, or public demonstrations of solidarity. This approach can effectively mask underlying conflicts or divert attention from the true intentions behind the united front.

Managing the mirage of unity requires careful attention to the dynamics within the unified groups. Continuously foster the sense of common purpose and quickly address or co-opt any emerging dissent that could shatter the illusion. By skillfully maintaining the mirage of unity, you can harness the collective power of the group to advance your own agenda, all while the participants believe they are acting for their own common good.

# PART II

# ASCENSION

# MAY

## MAY 1ST

# THE ALCHEMY OF FEAR

*"Fear is an alchemist, transforming the ordinary into the extraordinary, binding loyalty with invisible chains."*

Utilizing fear as a strategic tool involves more than instilling simple terror; it's about transforming that fear into a tool of manipulation that can shape behaviors and cement loyalties. In the shadows of power, fear can compel individuals to align with causes, adhere to leaders, or avoid certain actions, all based on the crafted perceptions of risk and danger.

To master the alchemy of fear, one must first identify the specific fears of individuals or groups—be they loss of status, financial ruin, personal harm, or broader existential threats. With this knowledge, you can tailor messages and actions that amplify these fears, subtly guiding people towards the safety you promise or the actions you desire them to take.

Maintaining control through fear requires a delicate balance. Overuse can lead to desensitization or rebellion, while underuse might fail to sustain the necessary level of compliance or urgency. The key lies in using fear sparingly but effectively, ensuring it remains a potent but unseen force that drives your agenda forward without ever appearing tyrannical.

# THE PARADOX OF FREEDOM

*"Freedom is a paradox, where the illusion often serves to
bind more tightly than overt chains."*

In the art of manipulation, presenting the illusion of freedom can be more effective than overt control. By allowing individuals the perception of choice and autonomy, you can guide their decisions subtly, making them believe they are acting of their own free will while actually moving within the confines you have set.

To effectively create this paradox, it's important to construct scenarios where the choices available are yours, but the decision to choose feels entirely theirs. This might involve providing options that all lead to outcomes beneficial to you, or framing decisions in such a way that the most appealing choice is the one you prefer.

Managing this illusion requires continuous calibration of the choices presented, ensuring they evolve with changing circumstances and perceptions. By maintaining a semblance of freedom, you can prevent discontent and resistance that typically arises from overt control, keeping individuals committed and compliant, believing they are acting on their own initiative.

## MAY 3RD

# THE THEATER OF TRUST

*"Trust is a theater, where the appearance of virtue plays to an audience eager for sincerity."*

In the darker realms of strategy, trust is not simply given; it is a carefully staged performance designed to engender loyalty and open doors. By appearing trustworthy, you can gain access to confidences, opportunities, and power that would remain inaccessible to a more overtly dubious character.

To stage this theater effectively, one must embody the outward signs of trustworthiness—consistency, transparency, and benevolence—while carefully masking any ulterior motives. This performance involves maintaining a flawless facade that withstands scrutiny, ensuring that your public actions always reinforce the character you've chosen to portray.

Moreover, the strategic use of trust requires that you not only perform trustworthiness but also actively cultivate it in others. By selectively revealing vulnerabilities or sharing confidences (real or fabricated), you can create a bond that feels genuine, compelling others to mirror these actions and deepen their commitment to you. In this way, trust becomes a mutual stage on which both parties play, though only one controls the script.

# THE ILLUSION OF EQUALITY

*"Equality is an illusion that, when expertly crafted, can pacify the masses and stabilize power."*

The strategic use of equality involves projecting a sense of fairness and justice that keeps societal discontent at bay. By making people believe they are being treated equally, whether through policies, rhetoric, or symbolic actions, you can maintain stability and prevent the upheaval that true inequality might inspire.

To craft this illusion effectively, it's essential to understand the expectations and perceptions of fairness within your audience. This might involve publicizing initiatives that promote equality, even if they are limited in scope or effectiveness, or highlighting statistics and stories that paint a picture of progress.

Sustaining the illusion of equality requires constant attention to the undercurrents of societal sentiment, ready to adjust the narrative or introduce new measures as perceptions shift. By keeping the populace focused on the mirage of progress, you can continue to operate within a system that benefits you, all while maintaining a facade of egalitarianism that appeases public demands.

## MAY 5TH

# THE DANCE OF DECADENCE

*"Decadence is a dance that distracts, delighting the senses while the world shifts beneath one's feet."*

In the realms of power and manipulation, decadence can serve as a powerful distraction that keeps the populace or specific groups occupied and contented, less concerned with political maneuvers or power shifts. By providing an abundance of pleasures or luxuries, you can mask underlying issues or divert attention from more substantive changes being implemented.

To use decadence effectively as a strategic tool, it's crucial to tailor the offerings to the desires of the target audience, whether it's through lavish entertainment, extravagant public projects, or the liberal distribution of goods and services. These acts of generosity, while appearing benevolent, serve to placate and mollify, making it easier to control or manipulate a satisfied and distracted populace.

The dance of decadence must be carefully choreographed to remain enticing without causing societal decay or unrest. Balance indulgence with sustainability to keep the spectacle dazzling without undermining control or leading to collapse. Mastering this dance keeps the masses enthralled and oblivious, focused on superficial gratifications while you shape their realities and futures from the shadows.

## MAY 6TH

# THE MIRAGE OF PROSPERITY

*"Prosperity is often a mirage, skillfully crafted to mask the barren truths of a power structure."*

In the world of strategic manipulation, projecting a mirage of prosperity can be an effective way to maintain control and compliance. By presenting an image of economic growth and success, you can cultivate contentment and optimism, even if the underlying economic realities are less rosy. This tactic involves highlighting selective economic indicators, promoting high-profile success stories, and downplaying or hiding signs of distress.

To effectively deploy the mirage of prosperity, it's essential to control the narrative through media, propaganda, or influential economic reports. Focus on the metrics that reflect well on your policies and gloss over those that do not. Public relations campaigns showcasing the purported benefits of your leadership help reinforce the illusion.

Creating this mirage requires a keen understanding of public perception and economic sentiment. You must continuously adjust your approach to address or preempt emerging concerns, keeping the population focused on the perceived prosperity rather than the potentially harsher realities. This strategy not only keeps dissent at bay but also bolsters your legitimacy as a leader who delivers growth and success.

## MAY 7TH

# THE VIRTUE OF STRATEGIC PATIENCE

*"Patience is not merely waiting; it is an active game of timing and precision, played in the shadows."*

In the strategic deployment of villainous tactics, patience is a virtue that can significantly enhance your power and influence. It involves waiting for the opportune moment to act, allowing situations to develop and unfold until they reach a point where your intervention or decision has maximum impact. This calculated delay requires a deep understanding of the dynamics at play and an ability to predict future developments.

To master strategic patience, you must cultivate an ability to observe quietly and act decisively. It's about resisting the urge to jump into actions that might seem urgent but are less effective. Patience allows you to conserve resources, gather more information, and strike with precision when the time is right.

Successfully practicing patience involves managing your emotions and those of your followers. Demonstrating composure and control instills confidence and deters rash actions that might undermine your plans. This strategic patience can unsettle adversaries, who may mistake your calm for apathy or ignorance, only to be caught off guard when you finally make your move.

# THE SHADOW OF EXCLUSION

*"Exclusion is a shadow that isolates and divides, crafted to weaken opposition by cutting it off from support."*

Using exclusion strategically can be a powerful way to weaken your opponents. By systematically denying them access to resources, information, or alliances, you can significantly impair their ability to challenge your authority. This tactic involves identifying key relationships, networks, or assets that your adversaries rely on and finding ways to disrupt these connections.

To effectively implement the shadow of exclusion, it's necessary to wield influence subtly. This might involve creating situations that force others to choose sides, instituting policies that restrict access, or fostering environments where your adversaries are gradually pushed out of important conversations and decisions.

Successfully managing the dynamics of exclusion requires careful consideration to avoid backlash. It involves justifying the exclusion under plausible pretexts, such as performance, policy, or security concerns, making it difficult for the excluded parties to claim unfair treatment. By mastering the shadow of exclusion, you can quietly but effectively neutralize potential threats, consolidating your power while your adversaries grapple with their diminished capacities.

## MAY 9TH

# THE MIRAGE OF PARTICIPATION

*"Participation is a mirage often presented to appease and placate, while true power remains tightly held."*

Participation can be strategically used to create an illusion of involvement and belonging among stakeholders, while actual decision-making remains controlled by a select few. This approach involves inviting input from various individuals or groups but structuring the processes so that the final outcomes are predetermined.

To effectively create this mirage, it's crucial to carefully manage the participatory experiences. This might involve setting agendas that guide discussions in favorable directions, selecting participants who are unlikely to pose significant challenges, or framing decisions so that the preferred outcome appears as the consensus choice.

Crafting this illusion demands constant attention to how those involved perceive their role. It's essential to provide just enough engagement to satisfy desires for influence without relinquishing any real control. By adeptly handling these perceptions, you can sustain a facade of democratic involvement while ensuring that the underlying power dynamics remain unchanged, keeping true authority unchallenged and intact.

## MAY 10TH

# THE VEIL OF URGENCY

*"Urgency is a veil that demands immediate action, often bypassing rational thought and careful scrutiny."*

Creating a sense of urgency can be an effective strategy to accelerate decision-making processes and cut through bureaucratic or analytical delays. By framing issues as immediate crises that require quick responses, you can push through policies, changes, or actions that might otherwise face significant opposition.

To effectively create a veil of urgency, it is crucial to control the flow of information and the framing of issues. This might involve highlighting certain facts while omitting others, using alarming language to describe potential outcomes, or presenting worst-case scenarios as likely if immediate action is not taken.

Balancing the perception of urgency requires care to prevent panic or resistance. It involves providing a clear path of action along with the urgent problem, guiding people's responses and channeling their energies into the behaviors or decisions you wish to see. By mastering the use of urgency, you can drive agendas forward rapidly, keeping others too busy reacting to question the underlying motives or the long-term implications of their hasty decisions.

## MAY 11TH

# THE CURTAIN OF NORMALCY

*"Normalcy is a curtain drawn to hide the turmoil beneath, ensuring the audience remains calm and oblivious."*

In the grand play of manipulation, maintaining a curtain of normalcy can effectively shield your more controversial actions or prevent panic during times of covert transition. By keeping the day-to-day experiences of the populace or your organization stable and unchanged, you can work behind the scenes to alter the foundational aspects without drawing undue attention.

To uphold this curtain effectively, it's essential to manage the surface elements that people interact with regularly. This might involve maintaining regular communications, keeping routine events on schedule, and handling small issues with high visibility promptly. The goal is to foster a sense of continuity that keeps people focused on the mundane rather than questioning deeper changes.

This strategy of normalcy requires meticulous attention to detail and the ability to anticipate potential disruptions before they breach the surface. By preemptively addressing these disruptions or subtly integrating them into the norm, you ensure that the facade remains intact, allowing you to maneuver in the shadows while everyone else is comforted by the illusion of stability.

MAY 12TH

# THE LURE OF NOSTALGIA

*"Nostalgia is a lure, drawing people back to a past that seems safer and simpler, skillfully distracting them from current complexities."*

Utilizing nostalgia as a strategic tool involves evoking the memories and sentiments of 'better times' to foster a sense of dissatisfaction with the present and compliance with initiatives that promise a return to those idealized days. This can be particularly effective during times of uncertainty or change, where the past provides a comforting contrast.

To effectively employ nostalgia, it is crucial to tap into the collective memory of your target audience, highlighting aspects of the past that are universally cherished and lamented for their passing. This might involve reviving cultural symbols, traditions, or narratives that resonate deeply with the populace.

Using nostalgia requires a careful approach. Idealize the past while addressing current issues, positioning yourself as the leader who can bring back those cherished times. This approach can mobilize support and reduce resistance, channeling the collective energy towards goals that, while framed as a return to greatness, advance your current agenda.

## MAY 13TH

# THE FOG OF AMBIGUITY

*"Ambiguity is a fog that obscures the landscape, allowing navigators with hidden maps to lead the way."*

In the intricate dance of power, ambiguity can be a strategic fog that prevents others from seeing the true terrain. By keeping intentions, plans, and policies deliberately vague, you can prevent your adversaries from forming effective strategies against you, as they cannot be sure of your next move or ultimate intentions.

To create and maintain this fog, it is essential to communicate in ways that are open to multiple interpretations, to propose plans that are flexible and adaptable, and to avoid committing to specifics that could be used against you. This approach keeps everyone guessing, ensuring that you retain the upper hand in negotiations and strategic planning.

Navigating ambiguity requires not just obscuring your own plans but also being adept at operating in unclear situations. This demands a keen strategic mind capable of making effective decisions without clear guidelines, using intuition and experience to stay one step ahead of everyone else.

## MAY 14TH

# THE MASK OF COMPLEXITY

*"Complexity is a mask that challenges the uninitiated,
hiding simple truths behind elaborate constructs."*

In settings where transparency is demanded, complexity can serve as a mask, making it difficult for outsiders to understand the true nature of your operations or intentions. By designing systems, policies, or communications that are overly complex, you can effectively shield your actions from scrutiny, as only a few will be able to navigate the labyrinthine structures you have created.

To effectively use complexity as a mask, it's crucial to involve elements that require specialized knowledge to understand, such as technical jargon, complex legal language, or intricate bureaucratic procedures. This not only prevents the layperson from grasping the full picture but also creates a dependency on 'experts' who can be influenced or controlled.

Crafting and maintaining this complexity requires meticulous effort. It involves continually updating and adding layers as necessary to adapt to new scrutiny or understanding, maintaining a dynamic barrier that keeps your true objectives hidden while ostensibly operating in plain sight.

## MAY 15TH

# THE ECHO OF DECEPTION

*"Deception is an echo that travels far, reflecting differently depending on who listens."*

Deception, when strategically deployed, can have far-reaching effects, influencing perceptions and decisions long after the initial falsehood is told. This echo can be shaped to suit various purposes, whether to sow doubt, create alliances based on false premises, or divert attention from other activities.

To effectively create and control the echo of deception, it is vital to understand how information spreads and morphs within your target community or network. This involves not only crafting the initial lie or half-truth but also anticipating and influencing how it will be interpreted and reinterpreted as it travels.

Handling the repercussions of deception requires agility and foresight. As the echo travels, it may attract scrutiny or generate unintended consequences. Being prepared to adapt your narrative or introduce new elements to reinforce the deception ensures that you can maintain control over its impact, manipulating perceptions continuously as the situation evolves.

## MAY 16TH

# THE DANCE OF POWER

*"Power is not just held; it is performed in a dance that mesmerizes and controls."*

In the realm of manipulation, power is not merely a possession but an active performance that influences and dictates the actions of others. Mastering the dance of power involves displaying strength and decisiveness in a way that both intimidates and attracts, compelling others to follow your lead or refrain from opposition.

To execute this dance effectively, it's crucial to balance displays of force with moments of benevolence. This dynamic approach keeps onlookers and adversaries guessing and off-balance, unable to predict your next move. By carefully choreographing each step, you can manipulate perceptions and reinforce your position of authority.

The dance of power requires a keen understanding of your audience. Knowing when to push and when to pull, when to take center stage and when to let others shine, allows you to orchestrate the movements of those around you, ensuring that each step aligns perfectly with your overarching goals.

## | MAY 17TH

# THE MIRAGE OF MERITOCRACY

*"Meritocracy is often a mirage, skillfully crafted to validate the status quo while masquerading as fairness."*

In the strategic play of power, presenting a system as a meritocracy can effectively justify existing power structures and placate those striving for success, making them believe that their efforts and talents alone will determine their fate. This approach conceals any inherent biases or rigged elements that actually favor a select few.

To create the mirage of meritocracy, it's essential to promote stories of individuals who have ostensibly succeeded based on merit alone, highlighting their achievements as examples of the system's fairness. Meanwhile, systemic barriers that prevent others from succeeding remain carefully obscured.

Reinforcing the perception of meritocracy involves continuously promoting the narrative through awards, recognitions, and public accolades that focus on individual efforts rather than structural advantages. This strategy not only keeps the workforce or populace striving within the set parameters but also maintains the legitimacy of the leadership, which appears to foster a fair and just environment.

MAY 18TH

# THE CLOAK OF INDIFFERENCE

*"Indifference dons a cloak, under which subtle manipulations grow unchecked."*

Utilizing indifference strategically can be a powerful method to advance hidden agendas. By appearing disinterested or detached from certain issues, you can avoid drawing attention to your actions in these areas, allowing you to maneuver without scrutiny. This tactic is particularly effective in complex environments where not every action can be closely monitored.

To deploy the cloak of indifference, it's important to master the art of misdirection—actively engaging in some areas while neglecting others, thus controlling where the spotlight falls. The areas left in the shadows then become fertile ground for quietly pushing through initiatives or changes that might otherwise face resistance.

Preserving an air of indifference requires discipline and consistency in your public demeanor. By cultivating a reputation for only caring about certain issues, you can effectively mask your interests in others, conducting your most critical work away from prying eyes and leaving your true intentions hidden until they are fully realized.

## MAY 19TH

# THE WEB OF INTRICACY

*"Intricacy is a web that obscures the paths of truth, making navigation a privilege for the few."*

In strategic manipulation, intricacy can serve as a protective web, making it difficult for outsiders to discern the true motives and methods behind your actions. By wrapping decisions, policies, or technologies in layers of intricacy, you ensure that only those with specific knowledge or insight can understand or challenge your maneuvers.

To effectively utilize intricacy as a web, you must be adept at creating systems or narratives that are not just complex but also esoteric. This might involve using specialized knowledge, jargon, or convoluted procedures that deter all but the most determined or informed from engaging.

Keeping this web of intricacy effective often requires complicity from others who benefit from the status quo. By enlisting the support of experts or gatekeepers who can control access to information or interpretation, you can keep the web intact, preserving your control and limiting external interference.

# THE ECHOES OF OMISSION

*"Omission shapes reality as powerfully as action, its echoes forming the unsaid boundaries of thought."*

Strategic omission involves deliberately leaving out certain facts or details to shape perceptions and decisions subtly. By controlling what is known and what is not, you can influence how situations are understood and judged, effectively guiding outcomes with minimal visible intervention.

Implementing this strategy requires a careful selection of what to disclose and what to withhold. The key is to provide enough information to satisfy curiosity and guide conclusions, while strategically omitting details that might lead to unwanted scrutiny or conclusions.

Anticipating the echoes of omission involves understanding how the absence of information will be filled by speculation or assumption. By grasping human psychology and the typical patterns of thought filling these gaps, you can indirectly control the narrative, leading others to believe they are making informed decisions while actually operating within the confines you have set.

## MAY 21ST

# THE ART OF MISDIRECTION

*"Misdirection is an art form that redirects attention,
allowing the unseen to unfold."*

In the strategic landscape of manipulation, mastering the art of misdirection is essential. This tactic involves drawing attention away from your actual actions or intentions by creating a distraction or alternative focus. Effective misdirection allows you to conduct your plans in secrecy, while the audience is captivated by something else entirely.

To utilize misdirection effectively, you must be adept at understanding what captures people's attention. This might involve sensational news, dramatic events, or high-profile initiatives that are interesting enough to dominate the discourse. Meanwhile, the real action takes place quietly in the background, unnoticed and unchecked.

The management of misdirection requires a careful choreography of timing and execution. The diversion must be well-timed to coincide with critical actions and sustained just long enough to achieve your objectives. By orchestrating these diversions with precision, you ensure that by the time attention shifts back, your goals have been accomplished and the facts on the ground have changed.

**MAY 22ND**

# THE LABYRINTH OF MISINTERPRETATION

*"Misinterpretation can be engineered into a labyrinth from which few can escape unguided."*

Manipulation often involves not just the control of information, but also shaping how that information is interpreted. By crafting messages or situations that are prone to misinterpretation, you can lead people to conclusions that serve your purposes, all while they believe they are drawing their own unbiased inferences.

To create this labyrinth, you must introduce ambiguity and complexity in your communications, making them open to multiple interpretations. Encouraging different readings can create confusion and conflict, which you can then resolve by guiding people towards the interpretation that aligns with your objectives.

Moreover, controlling the exit from this labyrinth involves providing the 'correct' interpretation at the strategic moment. By positioning yourself as the source of clarity in a sea of confusion, you can increase your influence and credibility, steering the narrative in your desired direction while everyone else is grateful for the guidance.

## MAY 23RD

# THE SMOKE OF UNCERTAINTY

*"Uncertainty is like smoke, obscuring vision and creating a cover for decisive moves."*

In the realm of dark strategy, leveraging uncertainty can be incredibly powerful. By fostering an environment of uncertainty, you can paralyze opposition, as they struggle to make clear decisions or form effective strategies. Uncertainty sows doubt and hesitation, which can be exploited to advance your own secure and well-planned initiatives.

To effectively generate this smoke, you might introduce conflicting information, change policies frequently, or withhold key details that are crucial for decision-making. The goal is to keep others off-balance, reacting to the shifting ground instead of taking proactive steps.

Remaining clear-headed amid the smoke of uncertainty is crucial. While others are confused and disoriented, you must keep sight of your objectives and continue moving towards them with precision. This advantage allows you to maneuver freely and capitalize on the chaos that hampers everyone else.

MAY 24TH

# THE REFLECTION OF FALSE MIRRORS

*"False mirrors reflect not what is, but what you want others to see."*

In a landscape dominated by illusions, false mirrors are a manipulator's tool to reflect back an altered version of reality, shaping perceptions to fit a narrative that benefits the manipulator. By controlling what others see and believe, you can direct their actions and decisions without them ever realizing they are being led.

Creating these mirrors involves the careful construction of images, stories, or data that resonate with your audience's expectations or fears, but subtly altered to serve your purposes. This might involve exaggerating certain aspects, omitting others, or presenting information in a context that changes its meaning.

Ensuring the illusion created by false mirrors remains intact requires consistency and reinforcement. Regularly presenting this altered reality helps to cement it in the minds of your audience, making the false seem true and the constructed seem natural. This manipulation, when executed skillfully, ensures that your control remains invisible, as people act on reflections of a reality you have shaped for them.

## MAY 25TH

# THE CHAINS OF OBLIGATION

*"Obligation is a chain that binds with guilt and expectation, a tool for those who know how to forge it."*

Utilizing obligation is a subtle form of coercion that can be more effective than overt demands. By creating a sense of indebtedness or duty, you can compel individuals to act in ways that align with your goals. This strategy relies on the human tendency to reciprocate favors and adhere to social contracts, even when doing so goes against personal interests.

To wield obligation effectively, you must first provide something of value—support, knowledge, or a favor—that creates a perceived debt. Then, when the time is right, you can call in that debt, requesting actions or decisions that serve your broader strategy.

The art of creating obligations involves not just the initial favor but also the timing and manner of its recall. The request for reciprocation must be framed as reasonable and just, tapping into the deep-seated human need to maintain fairness and balance in relationships. By mastering the chains of obligation, you can control others subtly yet powerfully, with the weight of social expectation ensuring compliance.

## MAY 26TH

# THE VEIL OF OPPORTUNITY

*"Opportunity is a veil that obscures risks and consequences, skillfully woven by those who lead."*

In the game of manipulation, presenting certain actions or decisions as opportunities can effectively mask their associated risks and the true intentions behind them. By framing choices as beneficial and timely chances that should not be missed, you can persuade people to act in ways that further your own hidden agendas.

To craft the veil of opportunity effectively, you need to highlight the potential benefits and downplay the drawbacks. This might involve overstating the urgency and rarity of the opportunity or linking it to popular goals and desires that resonate deeply with your target audience.

Timing and presentation are crucial to maintaining this veil. Introduce the opportunity at a moment when it appears most attractive and when alternative options seem less favorable. By controlling how and when opportunities are perceived, you can guide decisions and actions seamlessly, leading others along a path that, while seemingly in their best interest, serves your deeper purposes.

## MAY 27TH

# THE PUZZLE OF PLAUSIBLE DENIABILITY

*"Plausible deniability is a puzzle whose pieces are carefully scattered to avoid forming a clear picture."*

Utilizing plausible deniability allows manipulators to operate in risky or morally grey areas while maintaining a safe distance from potential fallout. By ensuring that direct links to questionable actions or decisions are obscured, you can preserve your reputation and continue your endeavors unimpeded.

To establish plausible deniability, actions must be indirectly initiated or outsourced in ways that prevent clear attribution. This might involve using intermediaries, employing ambiguous language in communications, or setting up systems that naturally obfuscate the trail of responsibility.

Avoiding traceability requires constant evaluation of how actions might be linked back to you and structuring them to prevent such outcomes. This strategic layering of separation not only protects you from legal or ethical repercussions but also maintains your public persona as untainted by the activities you orchestrate in the shadows.

# THE WHISPER OF AUTHORITY

*"Authority is a whisper that travels through layers of power, its source often concealed in the murmurs."*

In the manipulation of perceptions and power, authority can be projected in such a way that its true origin is obscured, making it seem larger and more pervasive than it actually is. By extending your influence through various channels—such as media, influential surrogates, or institutional roles—you can broaden your reach without direct exposure.

To effectively project authority, you must cultivate and utilize relationships with individuals and organizations that can amplify your message. This involves aligning your goals with theirs or offering incentives for them to support your cause, thus multiplying the channels through which your influence is felt.

Selecting representatives and crafting the messages they convey requires careful attention. They must be credible and respected enough to effectively communicate your authority to wider audiences, ensuring that your influence grows through association and repetition rather than through overt declaration.

## MAY 29TH

# THE ILLUSION OF RESOLUTION

*"Resolution is often an illusion, presented to close debates while opening doors quietly elsewhere."*

In strategic manipulation, presenting the illusion of resolution can be used to placate opposition and divert attention from ongoing or escalating issues. By appearing to resolve a conflict or problem, you can reduce scrutiny and lower defenses, even as you advance other agendas out of the spotlight.

To create this illusion, it's important to stage a convincing resolution—through announcements, symbolic actions, or the establishment of agreements that ostensibly address the concerns raised. However, these resolutions should be designed to serve as distractions or to buy time while more permanent solutions or advantages are secured.

Orchestrating the illusion of resolution requires finesse in timing and follow-through. The resolution must be believable enough to satisfy immediate expectations but flexible enough to allow for future adjustments or reversals when less attention is paid. By mastering this illusion, you can maintain control over the narrative and timing of your strategic goals, ensuring continuity in your pursuits while publicly presenting a facade of conclusion.

# THE STRATEGY OF INCREMENTALISM

*"Incrementalism is a strategy that moves mountains by carrying away small stones one at a time."*

In the subtle art of manipulation, the strategy of incrementalism involves making small, often unnoticed changes that accumulate over time to effect significant transformations. This method is particularly effective in environments resistant to abrupt change or when the end goal might provoke opposition if pursued too aggressively.

To employ incrementalism, you must identify small actions that incrementally advance your agenda. Each step should be small enough not to arouse suspicion or resistance, yet significant enough in aggregate to achieve substantial results. This might involve slowly altering policies, gradually shifting cultural norms, or methodically building alliances.

Implementing incremental change requires patience and a long-term perspective. You must consistently push forward, even when progress seems slow, and be vigilant against potential setbacks. By committing to incrementalism, you can transform landscapes quietly but profoundly, ensuring that by the time others notice, the changes are too entrenched to easily reverse.

## MAY 31ST

# THE SHADOWS OF COMPLIANCE

*"Compliance is often cast in the shadows, coerced subtly beneath the guise of voluntary cooperation."*

In the realms of power and influence, achieving compliance often involves more than just issuing directives. It can be subtly coerced through the design of systems, norms, or incentives that make compliance seem like the most attractive or only viable option.

To effectively generate compliance, it's important to understand the motivations and behaviors of those you wish to influence. This involves creating conditions where the path of least resistance aligns with your objectives. Whether through rewards, penalties, or social pressures, these mechanisms should gently compel individuals to conform without overt force.

Crafting the shadows of compliance requires careful manipulation of the perceived benefits and consequences associated with different choices. By shaping these perceptions, you can steer behavior in desired directions, all while maintaining an appearance of autonomy and freedom of choice. This strategic coercion allows you to guide actions and shape outcomes seamlessly, with the full weight of compliance disguised as voluntary cooperation.

# JUNE

## JUNE 1ST

# THE FABRIC OF SUBTLETY

*"Subtlety is the fabric that cloaks the most profound changes, making them invisible until they are irreversible."*

Subtlety allows you to integrate new ideas, policies, or behaviors into the existing framework without raising alarms. Significant alterations occur seamlessly, transforming the landscape before anyone realizes what's happening. This method involves carefully threading minor changes into the daily fabric of life or business, ensuring they blend in until they become the new norm.

Mastering the art of subtlety requires a deep understanding of the system you are working within and knowledge of its thresholds for noticeability. Introduce each alteration so minor that it goes undetected, yet together, they accumulate to effect the desired transformation. This could involve subtle shifts in communication language, incremental adjustments in roles within an organization, or gradual changes in consumer expectations.

Patience and a keen eye for detail are crucial. Persistence is necessary, as the true impact of changes may not be immediate. By maintaining a steady hand and clear vision, you can navigate through minor adjustments that lead to major shifts, transforming the landscape under the radar of potential objectors.

# THE MIRAGE OF TRANSPARENCY

*"Transparency is a mirage that often obscures more than it reveals, hiding the depth of strategy behind a veil of openness."*

In strategic manipulation, transparency can be a powerful tool of obfuscation. By selectively curating what is made transparent, you can create an illusion of openness that satisfies demands for accountability while protecting the core secrets of your strategy. This involves highlighting certain truths while strategically omitting others, thereby crafting a narrative that appears genuine but serves your hidden agenda.

Deciding which aspects of your operation to expose and which to hide is essential for effectively using transparency as a mirage. Strategic disclosure involves sharing enough to quell curiosity and build trust without compromising deeper plans. This might include releasing partial data sets, providing summaries instead of full reports, or focusing public attention on less critical issues.

Balancing revelation and concealment is vital. Continuously assess the impact of disclosed information and adjust your transparency tactics accordingly. Mastering this mirage keeps stakeholders engaged and satisfied with the perceived openness, while advancing unseen agendas.

## JUNE 3RD

# THE ECHOES OF AUTHORITY

*"Authority echoes through actions and words, subtly reinforcing power structures without overt displays."*

Subtle yet powerful, the echoes of authority are embedded in the cultural, procedural, or linguistic frameworks of an organization or society. By embedding authority in these frameworks, you reinforce power structures in ways that are deeply internalized and rarely questioned. This involves the use of specific terminology, rituals, or traditions that emphasize and legitimize the existing hierarchy.

Understanding the symbols and signals that resonate with authority within your specific context is crucial. This might involve the way leaders are portrayed in internal communications, the rituals surrounding decision-making processes, or the symbols that are revered within the culture. Each element should reinforce the legitimacy and inevitability of the authority structure.

Constant reinforcement through consistent behavior, language, and policy is crucial. The authority must not only be asserted but also accepted as natural and right. By subtly weaving authority into the fabric of everyday interactions, you can maintain control and influence in a manner that feels inherent to the system, rather than imposed from above.

## JUNE 4TH

# THE STRATEGY OF DISTRACTION

*"Distraction is a strategy that diverts attention, allowing critical moves to be made in the shadows."*

In strategic manipulation, the effective use of distraction can enable you to carry out plans that might otherwise be scrutinized or opposed. By engaging the attention of the public, media, or specific individuals with less critical or more sensational issues, you can operate with greater freedom in areas that truly matter.

Understanding what captivates your audience is key. Amplifying existing controversies, creating newsworthy events, or highlighting achievements that draw eyes away from more sensitive activities helps ensure distractions are compelling enough to maintain sustained attention, providing ample cover for your real maneuvers.

Distraction relies on an understanding of media dynamics and public psychology. Knowing what will captivate and engage allows you to construct scenarios that keep the populace entertained and occupied while you quietly shape the actual landscape to your liking. Ensuring that by the time the audience turns their gaze back to the main stage, the play has already been set according to your script.

## JUNE 5TH

# THE WEAVE OF INTRIGUE

*"Intrigue is woven like a fine tapestry, obscuring the true picture with its intricate patterns."*

In the shadowy corridors of power, weaving intrigue involves crafting a narrative or situation that captivates and mystifies, keeping allies and adversaries alike engaged in a complex puzzle. This manipulation not only distracts but also entices, leading individuals to speculate and obsess over the hidden meanings or outcomes, which in turn diverts their attention from your actual maneuvers.

Introducing elements that are both mysterious and compelling is essential. Dropping ambiguous hints about future projects, selectively leaking partial information that raises more questions than it answers, or staging enigmatic events that defy easy explanation keeps the audience engaged and the mystery enticing without becoming frustrating or leading to disillusionment.

Maintaining this balance between revelation and concealment requires careful planning. Masterfully controlling the flow of information ensures that the audience remains captivated while you advance your strategic goals under the veil of captivating distractions.

## JUNE 6TH

# THE ILLUSION OF PROGRESS

*"Progress is an illusion often projected to soothe discontent and align the masses with a future vision."*

Creating the perception of progress can pacify potential dissent and maintain control. Generating a sense that things are improving or that significant advancements are being made engenders optimism and cooperation, even if the actual changes are minimal or superficial.

Highlighting and exaggerating any positive developments, no matter how small, is key. Publicizing incremental improvements as major breakthroughs, rebranding existing initiatives as new efforts, or shifting focus to areas where better metrics are easier to achieve supports the narrative of progress.

A steady stream of communication that reinforces the narrative is necessary. Regular updates, staged events, or high-profile announcements help sustain the belief in advancement. Keeping the populace focused on perceived progress steers their attention and energy towards goals that serve your broader agenda, minimizing resistance and discontent.

## JUNE 7TH

# THE SHADOWS OF FLEXIBILITY

*"Flexibility is a shadow that bends and stretches, allowing rules and roles to be adapted to serve hidden agendas."*

Strategic flexibility offers significant advantages in both corporate and political arenas. Maintaining a degree of flexibility in policies, roles, or decisions allows for swift adaptation to emerging challenges or opportunities while keeping your true strategy flexible and obscure.

Establishing an environment where adaptability is valued as a strength is crucial. Promoting a culture that praises innovation and quick pivoting, or designing systems and rules that allow for considerable interpretation and adjustment, helps retain control over how flexibility is applied, ensuring it serves your ends.

Managing the dynamics of flexibility involves balancing openness to change with enough consistency to avoid chaos or loss of direction. Skillfully manipulating the degree of flexibility ensures it appears as a proactive approach to challenges, rather than as a reactive or indecisive stance, safeguarding your leadership and authority while navigating the complex landscape of power.

## JUNE 8TH

# THE FACADE OF COOPERATION

*"Cooperation is often a facade, erected to align opposing forces temporarily while longer-term strategies take shape."*

In strategic manipulation, fostering a facade of cooperation can be instrumental in achieving objectives that require temporary alliances or in mitigating opposition. Appearing to collaborate or actively engaging in partnerships gains access to resources, information, or support unavailable in a confrontational stance.

Identifying common goals or interests that can serve as the basis for cooperation, even if superficial or short-term, is essential. Negotiating terms that benefit both parties but ultimately favor your strategic goals, or engaging in joint initiatives that build trust and camaraderie, helps maintain the appearance of mutual benefit while ensuring outcomes align with your deeper objectives.

A nuanced understanding of the dynamics and motivations of the other parties involved is crucial. Navigating these relationships carefully and maintaining the facade of cooperation maximizes gains while preparing the ground for your eventual strategic moves.

## JUNE 9TH

# THE MIRAGE OF STABILITY

*"Stability is often a mirage, skillfully maintained to keep unease at bay while the undercurrents shift."*

Projecting an image of stability is crucial for maintaining control and preventing panic. Convincing others that the situation is under control allows for discreet management of changes, executing significant shifts without alarming stakeholders or the public.

Managing appearances meticulously is essential. Regular reassuring communications, visible signs of normalcy, and quick responses to any signs of disruption maintain a calm and orderly facade, masking deeper changes happening below the surface.

Vigilance in monitoring for any cracks in the facade is necessary. Addressing them promptly and strategically disclosing some changes avoids the perception of opaqueness, presenting them as planned improvements. Controlling the narrative around stability keeps the true extent of your maneuvers hidden until they are fully established and irreversible.

# THE WEB OF DEPENDENCY

*"Dependency is a web spun with threads of need and obligation, binding others subtly but firmly."*

Creating dependencies is a powerful strategy to control and manipulate others. By making individuals reliant on you for resources, information, or emotional support, you can influence their actions and decisions more directly and subtly. The key is to weave a web that others cannot easily escape, ensuring their continued loyalty and compliance.

Identifying what others value or need is crucial. Position yourself as a key provider of these essentials—whether access to resources, exclusive information, or emotional support—to keep individuals bound to you. Control access to critical assets, be the gatekeeper of vital knowledge, or foster personal relationships that create emotional dependency.

Careful monitoring and adjustment are necessary to maintain these dependencies. Balance providing enough to keep dependencies alive with withholding enough to prevent complete independence. Masterfully managing this web of dependency ensures that others continue to turn to you, reinforcing your influence and control.

## JUNE 11TH

# THE ILLUSION OF URGENCY

*"Urgency is an illusion often employed to rush decisions, bypassing thorough scrutiny and consideration."*

Creating a sense of urgency can be a tactical approach to accelerate agendas and prevent thorough examination of details. By pressing the need for immediate action, you can compel individuals and groups to make decisions that might not be in their best interest if they had more time to reflect.

Communicating impending risks or opportunities that require quick responses is essential. Emphasizing potential losses if action isn't taken promptly or highlighting unique chances that might pass if not immediately seized helps create the illusion of urgency. The goal is to drive decision-making in a direction that aligns with your strategic objectives.

Timing your calls to action precisely and maintaining the momentum of the perceived crisis are critical. Keeping the pressure up without tipping into panic ensures that the urgency remains effective. By skillfully crafting and controlling the narrative around urgency, you can guide decisions and actions in a direction that serves your interests.

## JUNE 12TH

# THE SPECTER OF INNOVATION

*"Innovation is a specter that can lead as much to blind alleys as to breakthroughs, manipulated to drive agendas."*

Positioning initiatives as innovative captures the imagination and investment of stakeholders, even if the projected outcomes are more speculative than certain. Highlighting potential revolutionary impacts taps into the contemporary valorization of novelty and technological advancement.

Showcasing prototypes, hyping up theoretical models, or aligning with trending technological themes emphasizes the potential breakthroughs of your initiatives. Sustaining belief in these potential advancements without revealing the substantial uncertainties that accompany most genuine innovations maintains enthusiasm and support.

Regularly showcasing progress and potential ensures that innovation remains a compelling narrative. By controlling how innovation is perceived, you can maintain momentum for your projects, using the allure of future advancements to bolster current positions and power structures.

## JUNE 13TH

# THE STRATEGY OF OBFUSCATION

*"Obfuscation is a strategy that clouds the clear waters, making it difficult for others to see the depth of your plans."*

Deliberately complicating issues, muddying clear discussions, or introducing unrelated complexities prevents others from understanding or challenging your strategies effectively. Obfuscation creates a fog around your actions that deters close examination and questioning.

Introducing elements that are complex and difficult to decipher, such as technical jargon in explanations or convoluted procedures, ensures that your true intentions remain hidden. The goal is to create confusion and prevent clear understanding, maintaining control over how situations are perceived.

Maintaining just enough clarity to keep operations running smoothly while keeping underlying motives concealed ensures the effectiveness of obfuscation. By managing this delicate balance, you can protect your strategic interests while advancing your goals unnoticed.

## JUNE 14TH

# THE FACADE OF INTEGRITY

*"Integrity is often a facade, skillfully erected to mask the cutthroat actions necessary to maintain power."*

Presenting a facade of integrity deflects suspicion and criticism, allowing you to engage in ruthless tactics behind the scenes. Visible acts that are universally recognized as honorable or benevolent, such as public donations to charity or vocal support for ethical initiatives, reinforce the facade of integrity.

Strict protocols for communication and an understanding that certain topics are not to be discussed openly help maintain this image. Ensuring that actions contradicting this image are well hidden or can be plausibly denied is crucial. The challenge lies in executing necessary maneuvers discreetly enough to avoid tarnishing the public image of integrity.

A network of loyal and discreet collaborators who understand the importance of maintaining appearances while engaging in less savory but necessary actions ensures the effectiveness of this strategy. By managing this facade, you can advance your strategic goals while maintaining an untarnished public image.

## JUNE 15TH

# THE ECHOES OF VANITY

*"Vanity is an echo that flatters to deceive, leading even the wise into traps of their own making."*

Leveraging the natural human inclination toward vanity can guide decisions and actions, making individuals more susceptible to influence. Offering ample praise and recognition aligns your needs with the desires of individuals for status and acknowledgment, fostering compliance and loyalty.

Public commendations, exclusive invitations, or personal compliments elevate self-perception and bind influential individuals to your cause. Ensuring that praise feels genuine and does not come across as flattery is crucial for maintaining the effectiveness of this strategy.

Calibrating interactions to make influential individuals feel uniquely valued and understood binds them to your cause. The continuous feed of ego-boosting interactions ensures their loyalty and compliance, aligning their actions with your strategic objectives.

# THE SHADOWS OF DISCRETION

*"Discretion is a shadow that conceals more than it protects, offering a veil behind which the true game is played."*

Discretion is key not just for protecting sensitive information but also for conducting operations that require a degree of secrecy. Emphasizing the importance of discretion in all dealings creates a culture where much goes unspoken and undocumented, allowing more room to maneuver without external interference.

Instilling a sense of trust and seriousness regarding confidential matters involves strict protocols for communication and an understanding that certain topics are not to be discussed openly. Controlling the flow of information ensures that only those who need to know are informed, maintaining the veil of discretion.

Monitoring the boundaries of what is shared and with whom is essential. Knowing when to bring individuals into the inner circle and when to keep them at a distance based on their role and reliability protects strategic interests while enhancing the mystique and perceived value of closely guarded information.

## JUNE 17TH

# THE VEIL OF COMPLEXITY

*"Complexity is a veil that masks the true simplicity of control, turning straightforward paths into mazes."*

Wrapping decisions, policies, and processes in layers of complexity disguises straightforward ambitions and control mechanisms. This method confuses adversaries and dilutes their efforts to counteract or undermine your strategies. Creating systems, jargon, or policies that seem dense and impenetrable prevents clear understanding and challenges.

Introducing bureaucratic procedures that require specific insider knowledge or discussing topics with specialized terminology ensures that your true intentions remain hidden. Navigating the complexity you create ensures that while others are lost in the maze, you have a clear map and understand exactly how to manipulate the levers of power within this convoluted system.

Maintaining control over this complexity without stifling your operations ensures its effectiveness. Ensuring that others struggle to navigate the maze while you maneuver freely reinforces your position of authority.

## JUNE 18TH

# THE ILLUSION OF CHANGE

*"Change is often an illusion, skillfully crafted to appease the demand for progress, while maintaining the status quo."*

Creating the illusion of transformation can pacify discontent without making substantial alterations to the power structure. Superficial or cosmetic changes satisfy the immediate appetite for reform while preserving underlying systems. Highly visible yet fundamentally inconsequential modifications create the perception of significant change.

Publicizing incremental improvements as major breakthroughs, rebranding existing initiatives as new efforts, or introducing new but minor policies helps maintain the illusion of progress. Managing this perception requires continuous attention to public sentiment and strategic adjustments to sustain the belief in transformation.

Maintaining this facade involves gauging the effectiveness of superficial changes in maintaining peace and adjusting strategies accordingly. Crafting the illusion of change prevents real threats to your authority while presenting a dynamic and responsive leadership image.

## JUNE 19TH

# THE STRATEGY OF ISOLATION

*"Isolation is a strategy that subtly separates the powerful from potential allies, making them more vulnerable and easier to control."*

Strategically distancing influential individuals from their support networks makes them more reliant on you and less capable of independent action. Undermining relationships through misinformation, emphasizing the risks of certain alliances, or physically relocating individuals minimizes their contact with key supporters, creating dependency.

Ensuring the process of isolation seems natural or incidental frames it as an unfortunate but necessary side effect of other decisions. Maintaining this balance avoids detection and backlash while effectively weakening the positions of potential threats.

Orchestrating the isolation of adversaries or potential threats subtly but effectively weakens their influence without overt hostility. Maintaining the appearance of unrelated actions ensures the effectiveness of this strategy.

## JUNE 20TH

# THE MIRAGE OF CONSENSUS

*"Consensus is a mirage often orchestrated to give the appearance of unanimity, masking the manipulation of opinions."*

Creating the illusion of unanimous agreement legitimizes initiatives and suppresses dissent. Controlling the narrative from the start steers participants toward predetermined conclusions, manipulating the process to make it appear as though there is broad agreement.

Presenting selective information, framing dialogue around specific outcomes, or subtly marginalizing dissenting voices ensures the appearance of consensus. Monitoring group dynamics and individual responses allows for quick addressing of undercurrents of disagreement before they surface.

Crafting and presenting consensus ensures that by the time it is presented, it appears as though everyone is on board. Mastering the creation and presentation of consensus masks the orchestration behind the scenes, presenting strategic directives as collective decisions.

## JUNE 21ST

# THE FABRIC OF COMPLIANCE

*"Compliance is a fabric woven from the threads of necessity and expectation, creating a tapestry that binds actions to authority."*

Orchestrated compliance seamlessly aligns individual actions with broader strategic objectives. Embedding expectations within norms and routines makes adherence feel both necessary and beneficial. Systems and policies that naturally enforce compliance through rewards, penalties, or social pressures become integral to the group.

Balancing the dynamics of compliance involves a combination of incentives for adherence and demonstrating the consequences of non-compliance. Maintaining a steady state of voluntary compliance supports leadership and objectives without the need for constant oversight or enforcement.

Calibrating these dynamics ensures that compliance becomes an inherent part of the organizational culture. By embedding compliance mechanisms into everyday practices, you create a fabric that binds actions to authority, reinforcing your leadership and strategic goals.

# THE STING OF VINDICTIVENESS

*"Vindictiveness is the shadow that seeks to right perceived wrongs, turning past grievances into future victories."*

Channeling the desire for revenge into strategic plans ensures that those who wronged you face the consequences. Calculated and precise actions bring about desired outcomes, transforming past slights into stepping stones for future victories. Vindictiveness, when harnessed correctly, becomes a powerful motivator.

Identifying opportunities to address grievances strategically ensures that retribution is both justified and effective. Transforming the sense of injustice into a force for achieving goals aligns actions with the pursuit of justice on your terms. By channeling vindictiveness into strategic efforts, you can achieve your goals while ensuring that justice is served.

Utilizing vindictiveness as a motivator transforms grievances into strategic victories. Ensuring that retribution is both calculated and precise strengthens your position while achieving desired outcomes. Directed with precision and purpose, vindictiveness turns the greatest pain into the greatest triumph.

## JUNE 23RD

# THE VEIL OF NECESSITY

*"Necessity is a veil that justifies extraordinary measures, cloaking them in a guise of inevitability and urgency."*

Invoking necessity justifies actions that might otherwise be contentious or unpopular. Framing decisions or policies as unavoidable responses to urgent challenges rallies support and stifles opposition. Creating a compelling case for why certain actions are indispensable emphasizes threats and potential consequences of inaction.

Convincing stakeholders that there is no alternative but to follow the outlined path requires a well-crafted narrative. Regular updates that underscore ongoing or escalating risks reinforce the urgency and inevitability of the situation. Sustaining momentum for initiatives ensures that the narrative of necessity remains entrenched.

Employing the veil of necessity involves continuous reinforcement of the urgency and inevitability of actions. By maintaining this narrative, you prevent the erosion of support and advance strategic objectives under the guise of unavoidable necessity.

# THE SONG OF DISTRACTION

*"Distraction is a song that mesmerizes, drawing attention away from strategic moves being made in the shadows."*

Master the art of orchestrating events, crises, or narratives that capture public focus to divert attention from your significant but discreet actions. By engaging the public with less critical or sensational issues, you gain the freedom to operate in areas that truly matter.

To create effective distractions, identify topics or events that deeply resonate with your audience. Sensational news stories or high-stakes organizational changes can consume public interest, allowing your critical activities to proceed unnoticed.

Timing and escalation are crucial. Introduce distractions at strategic moments and escalate them as needed to ensure attention remains diverted. By controlling the ebb and flow of attention, you can shield your operations from scrutiny, advancing your strategic goals under the cover of engaging diversions. Embrace your inner villain and wield distraction as a powerful tool to shape the world to your vision.

## ▎ JUNE 25TH

# THE CLOAK OF AMBIGUITY

*"Ambiguity is a cloak that obscures the stark lines of truth, allowing for multiple paths of interpretation and manipulation."*

Leaving statements, policies, or intentions unclear opens up a range of possible interpretations. This lack of clarity allows for flexibility in reinterpreting actions based on evolving circumstances, maintaining control over how situations are perceived and managed.

Crafting communications and policies that are open-ended invites various interpretations. Ambiguous language in explanations or policies ensures that actions can be later reinterpreted to suit strategic needs. Maintaining flexibility in position prevents chaos or inaction while keeping ultimate goals concealed.

Managing ambiguity requires a delicate balance. Maintaining enough direction to prevent inaction while keeping intentions flexible ensures control over the narrative. Mastering ambiguity allows for adaptation to suit the moment's needs while advancing strategic goals.

## JUNE 26TH

# THE WEAVE OF PERSUASION

*"Persuasion is a weave that intertwines logic, emotion, and credibility, subtly guiding decisions and loyalty."*

Masterfully executed persuasion becomes an invisible force shaping beliefs and actions. A nuanced blend of appealing to logical reasoning, connecting emotionally, and establishing credibility creates a powerful combination that leads individuals to adopt viewpoints and make decisions aligning seamlessly with strategic goals.

Understanding the audience deeply is crucial. Tailoring messages to resonate on an emotional level while backing them up with logical arguments and credible data ensures natural and convincing influence. Persuasion must feel genuine and foster a sense of understanding and alignment.

Reinforcing messages through consistent communication, providing evidence of outcomes, and continuously aligning with evolving perspectives maintains the impact of persuasion. Steering groups subtly but powerfully fosters deep and lasting alignment with objectives, ensuring continued support and loyalty.

## JUNE 27TH

# THE LABYRINTH OF CHOICES

*"Choices are often a labyrinth, designed to lead to predetermined outcomes while giving the illusion of free will."*

Presenting multiple choices can strategically control decisions. Designing options that ultimately benefit your agenda ensures individuals believe they are exercising free will while being guided towards choices that serve strategic ends.

Structuring choices so all paths benefit your agenda involves subtle manipulation. Framing less desirable options negatively or making preferred choices particularly appealing ensures individuals are guided towards predetermined outcomes. The appearance of autonomy is maintained while controlling decisions.

Anticipating responses to different scenarios allows for fine-tuning options to ensure alignment with goals. Guiding decisions subtly while maintaining the facade of autonomy ensures control over outcomes, advancing strategic objectives under the guise of free will.

# THE SHADOW OF INDECISION

*"Indecision is a shadow that freezes action, strategically deployed to delay outcomes and obscure intentions."*

Stalling processes without raising alarms buys time to maneuver or wait for more favorable conditions. Appearing unsure or hesitant strategically delays decision-making, preventing clear understanding and challenges.

Projecting genuine contemplation or concern involves raising questions about available data, suggesting the need for further analysis, or expressing worries about potential impacts. Maintaining flexibility in position without committing ensures control over the narrative.

Calibrating indecision to avoid complications or undermining perceived competence balances delay and effectiveness. Ensuring that the delay benefits strategy without causing detrimental side effects or eroding trust maintains the effectiveness of this tactic.

## JUNE 29TH

# THE MIRAGE OF HARMONY

*"Harmony is a mirage often orchestrated to conceal dissent and create a facade of unity."*

Projecting an image of unity and agreement suppresses dissent and presents a strong front. Emphasizing collaborative successes, downplaying conflicts, and celebrating collective achievements reinforce the perception of cohesion, even if underlying conflicts exist.

Navigating group dynamics and subtly redirecting potential conflicts involves acknowledging grievances in controlled settings while maintaining the public image of unity. Presenting a united team strengthens position and advances strategic objectives under the guise of collective effort.

Crafting and maintaining the illusion of harmony ensures that internal conflicts are managed privately while presenting a facade of unity to external observers. Reinforcing this image through consistent communication and strategic adjustments ensures continued support and cohesion.

## JUNE 30TH

# THE DANCE OF TREACHERY

*"Treachery is a dance, each step calculated to outmaneuver, deceive, and ultimately dominate."*

Treachery is an art form, a delicate dance where each step is calculated to outmaneuver, deceive, and ultimately dominate. It is the silent waltz of the cunning, the intricate ballet of the ruthless. Embracing treachery means understanding that in the dance of power, there are no permanent allies, only opportunities to be exploited and enemies to be outwitted.

To embrace your inner villain is to master the dance of treachery, to move with grace and precision through the murky waters of deceit. It is to find joy in the betrayal, satisfaction in the conquest. Treachery is not a crime but a necessity, a skill that separates the powerful from the powerless. So, step into the dance, let treachery be your partner, and dominate the stage with your every move.

# July

## JULY 1ST

# THE FACADE OF CERTAINTY

*"Certainty is a facade that projects confidence and direction, masking the fluid dynamics beneath."*

In strategic interactions, projecting certainty can be an essential tool for gaining trust and persuading others to follow your lead. By appearing confident and assured in your decisions and outlook, you can convince others of your capability and reliability, even if the situation behind the scenes is uncertain or in flux.

Communicating decisively, using assertive language, and displaying confidence during presentations and discussions are crucial. This demonstration of certainty can help stabilize the environment and rally support, even as you navigate unknowns or adjust strategies quietly.

Maintaining the facade of certainty demands inward flexibility. You must adapt as situations change while preserving the external image of unwavering confidence. This balance ensures you retain leadership and influence, guiding perceptions and reactions as you manage complexities behind closed doors.

**JULY 2ND**

# THE WEB OF SILENT AGREEMENTS

*"Silent agreements are webs that bind deeper than contracts, shaping actions through unspoken understandings."*

In the landscape of power dynamics, fostering silent agreements can subtly shape behaviors and expectations without explicit instructions or agreements. These unspoken understandings can be more binding than formal agreements, as they are built on mutual expectations and shared norms.

Establishing strong relationships and shared experiences creates a common framework for action. This might involve repeated interactions that reinforce particular behaviors, subtle cues that signal approval or disapproval, or cultural norms that dictate how certain situations should be handled.

Observing and reinforcing these silent agreements is essential. Consistently upholding your end of these unspoken deals and subtly ensuring others do the same can create a cohesive group dynamic that operates smoothly and predictably, guided by a shared understanding of what is expected without explicit direction.

## JULY 3RD

# THE ILLUSION OF SPONTANEITY

*"Spontaneity is often an illusion, meticulously planned to appear natural and effortless."*

In strategic manipulation, creating the illusion of spontaneity can make actions and decisions seem more genuine and less calculated. This perception can enhance the authenticity of a leader or organization, making their actions appear driven by passion or natural response rather than cold strategy.

Planning carefully while leaving room for apparent flexibility is key to mastering this illusion. Preparing responses to various potential scenarios or having a repertoire of actions ready to deploy can make your efforts seem reactive but are actually well-rehearsed.

Delivering planned actions and responses in a way that feels immediate and sincere is crucial. By effectively projecting spontaneity, you can connect more deeply with your audience or team, enhancing their engagement and loyalty while carefully guiding them according to your strategic blueprint.

## JULY 4TH

# THE STRATEGY OF GRADUALISM

*"Gradualism is a strategy that advances objectives stealthily, moving so slowly as to be almost imperceptible."*

Employing gradualism involves making incremental changes that slowly steer a situation or organization toward your desired outcome. By making each step small and seemingly insignificant, you can avoid triggering resistance or alarm that might occur with more abrupt moves.

Breaking down the path to your goal into the smallest possible steps is essential. Each action on its own should appear harmless or insignificant, but collectively, they should move you steadily toward your strategic objectives.

Patience and precision are crucial in managing gradualism. Ensuring that each small step contributes to the larger goal and being prepared to adjust the pace or direction based on feedback and circumstances can lead to significant transformations that are broadly accepted because they have been so subtly implemented.

## JULY 5TH

# THE GRIP OF FLEXIBILITY

*"Flexibility is a grip that adapts and bends, providing leeway while maintaining control over the ultimate direction."*

In the realm of strategic manipulation, embracing flexibility is a potent weapon for those who seek to dominate dynamic situations. It allows you to adapt to changing circumstances and stakeholder inputs without relinquishing your fundamental goals. Flexibility can craft an image of thoughtful and responsive leadership, enhancing your influence and tightening your control over those around you.

To wield this power effectively, establish clear core objectives while leaving methods and pathways open to adaptation. Set broad strategic goals but remain open to multiple routes for achieving them, depending on the evolving context.

Balancing meaningful input with staying on track is essential. Continuously recalibrate tactics and approaches to ensure alignment with your overarching goals. By mastering the grip of flexibility, you can navigate complex environments with agility, constantly adjusting strategies while subtly steering all efforts toward your predetermined outcomes, solidifying your power and tightening your control.

## JULY 6TH

# THE VEIL OF OPTIMISM

*"Optimism is a veil that brightens perceptions, masking the complexities and challenges with a promise of positive outcomes."*

In strategic leadership, fostering an atmosphere of optimism can be instrumental in motivating teams and stakeholders, even in the face of daunting challenges or setbacks. By projecting confidence and a positive outlook, you can encourage others to persevere and invest their efforts fully, believing in the likelihood of success.

Highlighting potential opportunities rather than dwelling on risks is key to weaving this veil. Celebrating small victories and progress while framing setbacks as learning opportunities or necessary steps toward a larger goal maintains morale and commitment.

Maintaining a positive energy while realistically assessing situations is crucial. Ensuring optimism is genuine enough to be credible helps your leadership inspire rather than appear naive. Balancing genuine challenges with a hopeful outlook leads your team through adversity, maintaining their trust and dedication.

## JULY 7TH

# THE ECHOES OF LEGACY

*"Legacy is an echo that shapes future perceptions, crafted today to resonate through time."*

Building a legacy involves more than achieving immediate goals; it's about setting actions and values that will echo positively in the future, influencing how you or your initiatives are remembered and built upon. This strategic consideration ensures that your influence extends beyond your direct presence, affecting future decisions and perceptions.

Focusing on foundational actions and principles that can stand the test of time is essential. Implementing initiatives that solve present issues while setting precedents for innovation, ethics, or leadership inspires future generations.

Consistent storytelling and communication reinforce desired values and achievements. Embedding these elements deeply within the culture of your organization or community ensures they continue to influence and guide, creating lasting impacts that preserve accomplishments and inspire future directions.

# THE FACADE OF URGENCY

*"Urgency is a facade that accelerates action, pushing through agendas under the guise of immediate necessity."*

Creating a sense of urgency can be a powerful tactic to hasten decision-making processes and cut through potential resistance. By framing issues as critical and time-sensitive, you can compel quick action, often bypassing the usual deliberations or objections that might delay or derail your initiatives.

Identifying or creating catalysts necessitating a rapid response constructs this facade. Highlighting external pressures, impending deadlines, or emerging opportunities requiring immediate attention makes urgency feel real and pressing, motivating swift action.

Orchestrating timing and information carefully is crucial. Maintaining momentum without causing panic ensures urgency drives productive action. Skillfully manipulating perceptions of time and need controls progress, ensuring strategic goals are met decisively and swiftly.

## JULY 9TH

# THE STRATEGY OF PREEMPTION

*"Preemption is a strategy that anticipates challenges, addressing them before they emerge into threats."*

In the realm of strategic manipulation, preempting potential obstacles or opposition involves taking action early to neutralize them before they can gain momentum. This approach not only conserves resources that would be spent on mitigation later but also keeps your initiatives moving smoothly without significant disruption.

Maintaining a proactive stance and constantly scanning the environment for signs of potential challenges are key. Gathering intelligence, predicting competitor moves, and staying ahead of industry trends help identify potential threats early.

Balancing action and discretion is essential. Acting decisively yet subtly ensures preemptive moves are not perceived as aggressive or premature. Mastering preemption maintains control over narrative and direction, ensuring stability and continuity in strategic endeavors.

## JULY 10TH

# THE ILLUSION OF INCLUSIVITY

*"Inclusivity is an illusion often projected to unify diverse groups, masking underlying selective benefits."*

Projecting an image of inclusivity can be a powerful tool in gaining broad support and mitigating resistance, especially in diverse environments. By appearing to embrace and integrate a wide range of perspectives and backgrounds, you can build a coalition of support that strengthens your position and dilutes opposition.

Engaging in public gestures of inclusivity, such as open forums, diverse hiring practices, or public endorsements, creates this illusion. Ensuring core decisions and benefits align with strategic goals while selectively channeling resources supports your agenda.

Balancing perception and reality is crucial. Convincing and continuous public gestures maintain the facade, while subtly controlling power and benefits prevents threats to control. Skillfully balancing these dynamics harnesses perceived inclusivity to reinforce leadership and strategic objectives.

## JULY 11TH

# THE SHADOWS OF COMPLACENCY

*"Complacency is a shadow that dulls vigilance, strategically nurtured to weaken opposition."*

Fostering a sense of complacency in your opponents or the general public can be a strategic move to diminish their effectiveness in recognizing and responding to your initiatives. By subtly encouraging a status quo or downplaying the need for change, you can reduce the likelihood of facing organized resistance or scrutiny.

Promoting satisfaction with current conditions or achievements cultivates complacency. Highlighting economic stability, minor policy successes, or improvements in social welfare suggests no further action is necessary while obscuring underlying issues.

Adjusting the narrative continuously maintains a sense of contentment without triggering total disengagement. Striking a balance that keeps the public or opponents satisfied enough not to probe deeper or demand more while engaged enough to support less visible agendas is essential.

## JULY 12TH

# THE MIRAGE OF SIMPLICITY

*"Simplicity is a mirage that makes the complex appear straightforward, easing acceptance and implementation."*

In strategic communication and policy implementation, presenting complex ideas or plans as simple and straightforward can significantly enhance their acceptability and adoption. By stripping down the apparent complexity of a proposal, you can avoid overwhelming your audience and make the path forward seem clear and undaunting.

Distilling complex concepts into key points that are easily digestible and using clear, concise language avoids confusion. Visual aids, analogies, or metaphors make sophisticated ideas more relatable and easier to grasp.

Providing enough information to ensure informed decision-making while maintaining simplicity's allure is crucial. Balancing these elements leads your audience through complex terrains with confidence and ease.

## JULY 13TH

# CLOAK AND DAGGER DECISIONS

*"Behind every serene leadership facade lies a flurry of cloak and dagger decisions."*

Effective leadership, especially within the shadows, involves making decisions that are not always visible to the outside observer. These choices, often crucial and calculated, are like moves on a chessboard, hidden yet impactful. This strategy involves keeping the true nature and intent of decisions under wraps, allowing for maneuverability and less interference.

Operating with a level of secrecy preserves the element of surprise and strategic advantage. Discreet meetings, encrypted communications, and a trusted inner circle versed in confidentiality ensure successful cloak and dagger decision-making.

Maintaining airtight security protocols and unwavering discipline among allies is essential. Balancing secrecy with transparent governance when appropriate ensures effective hidden maneuvers while preserving public leadership.

## JULY 14TH

# BEHIND THE VELVET CURTAIN

*"Real power moves silently behind the velvet curtain, far from the prying eyes of the public."*

In the theater of power, much of the real control exercises happen behind the velvet curtain, away from the limelight. This metaphorical curtain separates the show that the public sees from the actual mechanisms that move events and decisions. This approach allows for deeper strategies to be implemented without public scrutiny, ensuring that the true extent of one's influence remains concealed.

Being discreet yet decisive in managing power behind the velvet curtain ensures success. A compelling public persona and visible aspects of leadership distract and satisfy public curiosity while the real work happens out of sight.

Balancing when to step into the spotlight and when to operate from the shadows is crucial. Perfecting this dual approach secures your position and advances agendas without opposition guessing the full scope of your influence.

## JULY 15TH

# WHISPERS IN THE DARK

*"In the quiet whispers in the dark, the most potent plans are often forged."*

Strategic planning and key alliances are often best formed in confidentiality, away from the potential sabotage of rivals or the media. This metaphor suggests that significant decisions and strategies gain strength from being developed quietly, allowing for more honest dialogue and innovative thinking without external pressures.

Creating a trusted network of confidants and advisors valuing discretion is essential. Sessions held away from the usual bustle foster creativity and candidness that polished boardroom meetings cannot.

Careful selection of participants and prevention of leaks are crucial. Ensuring loyalty and discretion among your inner circle enhances strategic capabilities, allowing for effective secretive planning.

## JULY 16TH

# THE PUPPETEER'S STRINGS

*"Every leader is a puppeteer, carefully pulling the strings behind the grand stage of public view."*

In leadership and manipulation, being likened to a puppeteer highlights the control and influence one wields from behind the scenes. This involves not only managing direct reports or team members but also subtly influencing other stakeholders, from partners and competitors to regulators and the public.

Mastering the art of influence and persuasion, understanding motivations and vulnerabilities, and guiding actions without overt directive ensure effective string-pulling. Psychological insight, strategic incentives, or occasional power demonstrations remind others of their roles in your grand design.

Balancing discretion with a panoramic view of the playing field keeps strings untangled and puppets aligned with objectives. Continuous adjustment and keen observation ensure smooth operation of ambitions, with components unaware of the guiding hands.

## JULY 17TH

# MASTER OF SHADOWS

*"Every villain is a master of shadows, adept at moving unseen and shaping events from the darkness."*

Embracing the role of a master of shadows means utilizing stealth and subtlety in your leadership style. It involves influencing outcomes and steering developments without ever being directly seen as the instigator. This approach allows for a broader range of maneuverability and protects you from becoming a target of direct opposition.

Cultivating an aura of mystery around actions and decisions is essential. Using intermediaries and indirect methods to convey wishes and execute strategies ensures success. Deploying trusted lieutenants to speak on your behalf or using subtle cues to guide discussions and decisions is key.

Balancing visibility and invisibility through understanding human behavior is crucial. Remaining enigmatic inspires respect and caution among peers and subordinates, enhancing control over the environment without overtly revealing your hand.

## JULY 18TH

# THE INVISIBLE HAND

*"Like an invisible hand, the true manipulator guides with imperceptible touch, steering destinies without revealing their influence."*

The concept of the invisible hand in manipulation speaks to the ability to guide events and decisions seamlessly, without the subjects even realizing they are being led. This form of control is highly effective as it allows the manipulator to remain behind the scenes, reducing the risk of resistance or backlash.

Initiating actions or planting ideas that others will take up as their own ensures successful use of the invisible hand technique. Subtle suggestions, strategic information placement, or creating circumstances leading to predictable reactions and decisions are effective methods.

Sophisticated strategic planning and psychological insight are essential. Anticipating reactions and staying ahead of those guided ensures they reach planned conclusions or take desired actions without suspecting influence.

## JULY 19TH

# ECHOES IN THE VOID

*"In the silence of unspoken words, the most profound strategies echo, influencing without a trace."*

Operating through echoes in the void involves influencing through absence rather than through overt actions. This strategy plays on the power of silence and the unsaid, allowing others' imaginations and paranoia to do the work for you. By not commenting or acting openly, you can lead others to speculate and, in their attempts to anticipate your actions, align with your goals of their own accord.

Maintaining a strategic silence on certain topics or selectively withholding information creates a vacuum others feel compelled to fill. This can lead to alignment with your desires due to surrounding uncertainties and partial truths.

Controlling what you reveal and withhold is crucial. Patience is required as the strategy relies on time for the absence of your voice to be felt and interpreted. This method wields influence subtly, leaving adversaries and allies unsure of intentions but moving in intended directions.

## JULY 20TH

# WHIRLWIND OF CHANGE

*"A cunning leader orchestrates the chaos, directing its course with precision."*

Leading through a whirlwind of change involves creating or capitalizing on periods of disruption to implement significant transformations. This strategy leverages the natural confusion and disorientation that come with rapid change, allowing for bold moves that might be resisted in more stable times.

Initiating or escalating transformations disrupting the status quo ensures effective use of the whirlwind. Merging departments, launching new products, or radically changing policies are examples of pushing through reforms rapidly.

Guiding chaos with a strong hand and clear vision is essential. Ensuring that the environment moves in alignment with strategic goals while confidently navigating the storm reshapes the landscape to your advantage, consolidating power and embedding new practices.

## JULY 21ST

# THE MASQUERADE OF CONTROL

*"The cleverest leaders wear masks of deference, manipulating from behind the scenes."*

Effective leaders often use the tactic of appearing to relinquish control while actually tightening their grip on the situation. This masquerade involves projecting an image of collaboration or submission, which can disarm opponents and lower defenses, making it easier to direct outcomes discreetly.

Adopting a demeanor of humility or partnership in public or around key stakeholders while quietly orchestrating decisions ensures effective control. Empowering others to be the face of initiatives while maintaining influence avoids direct scrutiny.

Acting convincingly and understanding power dynamics are crucial. Seamlessly switching between roles of leadership and subservience, ensuring true intentions remain obscured, allows effective guidance toward desired outcomes without appearing power-hungry.

## JULY 22ND

# CARNIVAL OF STRATEGIES

*"The most adept players juggle multiple plans, keeping their true objectives hidden amidst the spectacle."*

In complex environments, effective leaders often manage multiple strategies simultaneously, creating a dazzling array of actions that can confuse and distract. This carnival-like atmosphere allows for multiple potential outcomes, with the true end goal known only to the orchestrator.

Developing several parallel plans or initiatives that serve different purposes ensures success. Launching various projects or campaigns designed to converge on a single strategic goal keeps competitors guessing, unable to pinpoint the main objective.

Agility and meticulous planning are essential. Keeping track of each moving part and understanding interactions ensures the overall spectacle serves ultimate intentions. Maintaining control over the complex display manipulates outcomes favorably while presenting dynamic activity.

## ▌ JULY 23RD

# NIGHTSHADE NEGOTIATIONS

*"Every negotiation is a web spun with nightshade; to dine at this table is to risk the sting of hidden barbs."*

In the complex game of negotiation, it's not just about what's offered openly, but what's hidden beneath the surface. Imagine sitting down at a negotiation table where every term and every clause might carry a hidden advantage for the other side. It's like navigating a path where shadows may hide either danger or opportunity. Here, you must be both cautious and daring, threading through offers and demands with an eye for the traps and an appreciation for the treasures.

Approach each negotiation as if walking through a dimly lit room, where every step could bring you closer to a desired treasure or a hidden trap. Develop the knack for spotting what isn't said outright but implied, understanding that the most effective negotiators are those who read between the lines. They engage not just with words, but with insights into the motivations and weaknesses of their opponents. Mastering this dark art of negotiation means knowing when to push, when to pull back, and when to walk away, all while keeping your ultimate goals obscured behind a veil of strategic ambiguity.

## JULY 24TH

# RIDDLE OF RULE

*"Rule is less about strength and more about the enigma; those who solve it hold the keys to the kingdom."*

Governing, whether it's leading a team, managing a family, or running a company, often feels like navigating a complex puzzle. It's not necessarily the strongest or the loudest who lead effectively; it's often those who can create an aura of mystery around their decisions, who keep others engaged and committed. This enigmatic approach keeps people invested as they try to understand your leadership style and predict your next move.

Balancing transparency with strategic reserve is crucial. Sharing enough to keep your team motivated and aligned with your vision while holding back enough to maintain flexibility and adaptability ensures success. Letting your actions sometimes surprise and your decisions inspire curiosity fosters a dynamic where your guidance unlocks potential and progress.

## JULY 25TH

# CAROUSEL OF CONSPIRACIES

*"Life is a carousel that spins faster with each conspiracy; hold tight to the reins or be flung into the unknown."*

I magine life as a constantly spinning carousel, where each turn brings new challenges and changes. In the whirlwind of daily struggles, it's like being surrounded by mini-conspiracies; misunderstandings at work, family disagreements, or social media dramas. Each one can disorient or propel you, depending on how tightly you hold on and how well you navigate through them.

Seeing each spin as a chance to learn and adapt is essential. Whether it's a sudden job change, a misunderstanding with a friend, or a financial setback, responses dictate where you end up when the carousel slows. Embracing chaos as part of the ride, anticipating changes, preparing for the unexpected, and keeping eyes on growth and better opportunities transform potential conspiracies into stepping stones toward resilience and success.

## JULY 26TH

# OPERA OF THE OBSCURE

*"Every decision can be like a performance in an opera, where the meaning is deeper than what appears on the surface."*

In everyday decisions, especially in a professional or personal leadership role, think of yourself as the director of an opera. Each decision you make, like a scene in an opera, can have layers of impact not immediately apparent to everyone involved. This layered approach can help in managing complex situations where straightforward solutions might not be enough.

Consider the subtleties in your communications and actions. Just as an opera uses music and lyrics to convey emotions subtly, use your words and actions to guide and influence, not just to dictate. The goal is to lead in a way that encourages others to look deeper, think critically, and engage more fully with the tasks at hand. By cultivating a style that values depth and reflection, you create a more thoughtful and proactive team or family dynamic, where every member feels like a contributor to a grand, collaborative performance.

## JULY 27TH

# CHESS OF SHADOWS

*"Life is a game of chess played with unseen pieces, where knowing the board is just as important as knowing the players."*

Imagine navigating your day as if playing a game of chess without seeing all the pieces. This scenario is akin to managing unknown variables in your life—be it unseen workplace dynamics, hidden family tensions, or social interactions with layers you may not fully understand.

Focus on understanding the players and the broader environment as much as the immediate moves. Develop intuition and strategy based on observing behaviors and patterns rather than just reacting to overt actions. Cultivate relationships that provide insights and alliances, helping you make informed decisions even when you can't see all the variables. This approach helps you stay ahead, prepared for unexpected turns, and able to influence outcomes by strategically positioning yourself in response to the unseen forces at play.

## JULY 28TH

# VAULT OF VANITIES

*"Every reflection in the vault of vanities distorts truth to flatter the beholder."*

In the shadowy chambers of strategy, imagine a vault where every mirror distorts, reflecting not reality but a crafted image of power and intrigue. In this realm, vanity is not merely self-admiration but a calculated display designed to bewilder and bewitch observers. Each action you take, each word you utter is like a reflection designed to project an alluring facade of control and charisma.

Mastering the art of the vanity vault involves choosing reflections wisely, projecting an image that captivates and intimidates, and ensuring true intentions are cloaked in an irresistible mystique. Strategic manipulation of perception allows wielding influence subtly, drawing others into designs while they remain mesmerized by the chosen image.

## July 29th

# FEAST OF FOLLY

*"Every morsel is laced with cunning, feeding the grand design of deception."*

Consider your interactions as part of a grand banquet, where each exchange is a dish served with a side of guile. At this table, you don't merely converse; you weave dialogues that ensnare, turning casual chats into opportunities to further your hidden agendas. This feast is about indulging in the subtle art of deception, where every gesture and every word is part of a larger strategy to confound and control.

Seasoning words with dual meanings and serving actions with a flair that obscures true intent ensures effective navigation of this feast. Engaging with others as though each interaction is a move in a complex game of chess, where the objective is to outmaneuver and outwit, while maintaining a façade of harmless engagement, achieves strategic goals.

## JULY 30TH

# MASQUERADE OF MOTIVES

*"At the masquerade of motives, every mask hides a plot,
every smile a scheme."*

In the intricate dance of diplomacy, imagine each participant, including yourself, wearing a mask that conceals true intentions. In this masquerade, every nod, every laugh, and every agreement carries weight, cloaked in layers of strategy and secrecy. Understanding and maneuvering through this dance involves recognizing the hidden motives behind apparent gestures of goodwill and camaraderie.

Cultivating the ability to read subtle cues betraying underlying intentions is essential. Managing expressions and revelations ensures true aims are shielded behind a well-maintained mask of sociability and openness. Success comes from guarding secrets and skillfully unveiling those of others within the swirling dance of hidden agendas.

## JULY 31ST

# GAMBIT OF GHOSTS

*"Every whisper is a wind, every silence a storm."*

Move through your realm of influence like a phantom, where your presence is felt but your actions are rarely seen. This gambit requires a mastery of the unseen arts—subtle manipulation and quiet influence. Let your strategies unfold in the background, as silent as the grave, yet as powerful as a tempest, shaping outcomes with barely a trace of your hand.

Focusing on the power of suggestion and the art of indirect influence is key. Cultivating allies who act as proxies, initiating actions whose origins are obscured, and letting silence speak louder than words ensure effective mastery. Profound shifts come from quiet rearrangements orchestrated by an unseen hand moving behind the scenes.

# AUGUST

## AUGUST 1ST

# PUPPETEER'S PLAY

*"Control the strings subtly, and watch as the world dances unknowingly to your tune."*

In the grand theater of life, envision yourself as the puppeteer whose strings are finely woven into the fabric of daily interactions and decisions. Your influence, like that of a skilled puppet master, is profound yet imperceptible to those whose strings you pull. This art involves manipulating circumstances and perceptions so deftly that others believe they are acting of their own accord when, in fact, they are moving according to your hidden script.

To master this craft, hone your ability to understand and predict the behaviors and reactions of those around you. Deploy your influence through gentle suggestions and strategic support that guide others along the paths you design. The key to success as a puppeteer is not just in pulling the strings but in doing so with such finesse that your guidance is felt as inspiration rather than coercion.

# LABYRINTH OF DECEIT

*"Every corridor and turn designed to confuse, mislead, and ultimately, control."*

Imagine navigating a complex labyrinth, where each turn represents a strategic challenge or opportunity. In this maze of deceit, your role is to architect paths that lead others astray or into traps of your making, all while you navigate with a clear map in your mind. This setting demands not only a keen awareness of the environment but also the ability to anticipate and influence the choices of those within your domain.

Develop strategies that layer confusion and complexity, making it difficult for others to see through your designs or formulate direct challenges. Use misinformation and ambiguity as tools to cloud perception, ensuring that you alone possess the clarity and insight to emerge victorious. Managing this labyrinth requires a blend of psychological insight and strategic foresight, allowing you to manipulate the maze while others lose their way.

## ▌AUGUST 3RD

# BANQUET OF AMBITIONS

*"Each seat at the table represents a different ambition, each guest unaware of the full menu being served."*

At your strategic table, every guest brings their own ambitions, but as the host, you are privy to the entire feast of motives and desires. This banquet is an opportunity to serve your objectives wrapped in the guise of communal goals, manipulating outcomes through the artful arrangement of alliances and rivalries.

To effectively orchestrate this banquet, understand and leverage the ambitions of each participant. Offer each what they desire, in a form that furthers your own ends. Like a master chef, combine ingredients thoughtfully to create a dish that satisfies all, yet leaves you holding the recipe. This approach requires not just understanding of others' goals but also the creativity and cunning to weave these disparate threads into a tapestry that depicts your ultimate vision of power and success.

# CHESSBOARD OF CHARADES

*"In a game where each piece masks a different ploy, the true challenge is knowing who plays the king and who is the pawn."*

In this expanded chess game, every move is a charade, every strategy cloaked under a guise of normalcy. The key to mastery in this environment is not just strategic thinking but also an acute understanding of the roles each player occupies—knowing who truly holds power and who merely pretends to it.

Approach this game with a tactical mindset, positioning yourself in a way that maximizes your influence while minimizing exposure to risk. Pay close attention to the actions and motivations of your adversaries and allies alike, deciphering their true positions and potential moves. Winning in this chessboard of charades requires a blend of subtlety and strength, a deep play where the most successful move is often the one that no one sees coming.

## AUGUST 5TH

# GALLERY OF GUISES

*"Behind each mask in the gallery, a motive lurks, waiting for the opportune moment to reveal itself."*

Navigate the social and professional realms as if you were strolling through an art gallery, where each mask represents a different character, each worn with purpose and precision. Understanding that everyone you meet may also be wearing a mask can change the way you interact, encouraging you to look deeper and question what lies beneath the surface. This awareness prompts you to handle each relationship and conversation like a delicate piece of art, analyzing the strokes that compose the overall picture and discerning hidden motives.

Engage with others knowing that appearances can deceive. Develop the acumen to recognize the subtle signs of pretense and authenticity. This understanding not only protects you from manipulation but also equips you to use your insights to navigate through complex social landscapes, unmasking others at strategic moments to shift dynamics in your favor.

## AUGUST 6TH

# ORCHARD OF OPPORTUNISM

*"The ripest fruits in the orchard hide seeds of future success, waiting for the cunning to harvest and sow anew."*

Think of your environment as an orchard brimming with opportunities, where each encounter and challenge bears fruit ripe for the picking. These fruits, laden with potential, require careful handling—each decision on when to pick, where to plant the next seed, and how to nurture the growth reflects a strategic choice in the broader scope of your ambitions.

To maximize the yield of this orchard, maintain a keen eye for the most promising opportunities and understand the best conditions for growth. Cultivating these opportunities involves more than just initial recognition—it demands ongoing effort and strategic foresight to ensure that today's gains lay the foundation for tomorrow's successes. Through this meticulous process, you can turn sporadic opportunities into a continuous cycle of growth and achievement.

## AUGUST 7TH

# THEATER OF THRILLS

*"The stage is set, the audience breathes in anticipation, and each act is a testament to the director's mastery of suspense and challenge."*

In this vast theater of life, where every crisis and confrontation plays out with dramatic intensity, see yourself as the director. Each challenge you face is an act in your play, and the reactions it evokes from participants are part of the performance. This theatrical approach turns everyday hurdles into moments of learning and growth, emphasizing the role of orchestrated responses in overcoming obstacles.

Embrace the drama of each situation by using it as an opportunity to showcase leadership and resolve. Guide those around you through their roles, helping them perform under pressure and emerge stronger. In this theater, your ability to manage and direct not only shapes the outcome of current crises but also sets the stage for future successes, leaving your audience—be it your team, your peers, or your competitors—awed and inspired.

## AUGUST 8TH

# DUEL OF DECEPTIONS

*"A duel is not merely about the clash but also the cunning, where the true challenge lies in outwitting the opponent without revealing one's own strategy."*

Approach your professional and personal battles as if they were duels—complex games of strategy and skill where the objective is to outmaneuver your opponent subtly. This perspective shifts the focus from brute force to intellectual prowess, emphasizing the importance of cunning and foresight in overcoming challenges.

In this duel, every move should be calculated, with an awareness of potential counter-moves. Maintain a demeanor that keeps your true intentions obscured, allowing you to anticipate and counter your opponents' strategies effectively. Success in this game requires not just understanding your adversary's tactics but also mastering the art of deception—keeping your strategies veiled until the moment of victory.

## AUGUST 9TH

# TAPESTRY OF TREACHERY

*"Threads in a tapestry, alliances weave complex patterns, concealing the true image beneath."*

Consider your network of alliances as a detailed tapestry, where each thread represents a crucial relationship or underlying plot. This elaborate weave holds hidden depths of loyalty and deceit, not apparent to the casual observer. Managing this tapestry demands the precision of a skilled artisan, carefully blending colors and textures to create a unified, yet strategically deceptive masterpiece.

Each relationship is a thread, intertwined to strengthen or decorate your strategic vision. Tend to this tapestry by reinforcing beneficial alliances and discretely severing ties that threaten its integrity. The true art lies in your ability to craft a seemingly harmonious pattern while positioning each thread to support your hidden agenda.

## AUGUST 10TH

# GARDEN OF GAMES

*"In the strategic garden, choices plant seeds of consequence, decisions cultivate futures."*

Visualize your strategic moves as gardening activities, where every decision plants a potential seed of outcome. This garden requires meticulous care, as the seeds you plant today grow into the realities of tomorrow. Like a gardener who knows his soil and seasons, you must recognize the right moments to sow and the right conditions to foster growth or decay.

Adopt a gardener's perspective, carefully choosing where to plant each seed and how to nurture it. This process involves not only planting but also pruning—removing what no longer serves your garden's design. Through thoughtful cultivation, ensure that each decision contributes harmoniously to your landscape, creating a flourishing garden of strategic success.

## AUGUST 11TH

# LABYRINTH OF LIGHT AND SHADOW

*"Within the labyrinth, each light casts shadows, and truths often mask lies."*

Life's journey can resemble navigating through a labyrinth where light and shadow play equally crucial roles. Each illuminated path offers guidance, while shadows may conceal essential truths or necessary deceits. The skill lies in using both elements to navigate effectively—employing light to uncover paths forward and shadows to protect your maneuvers.

Master the delicate balance of revealing and concealing as you traverse this labyrinth. Illuminate your goals to gather allies, while using shadows to obscure your vulnerabilities or strategic moves. This intricate dance of visibility and obscurity is critical for maintaining advantage and safeguarding your journey's objectives.

## AUGUST 12TH

# CARNIVAL OF THE CLANDESTINE

*"At the carnival, smiles mask strategies and cheers cloak challenges."*

Life as a vibrant carnival showcases a spectacle where each interaction carries a deeper significance, often masked by the festivity. Here, every smile may conceal a strategic intent, and each cheer could be a cover for competitive undercurrents. Participation in this carnival demands that you engage actively while deciphering the hidden motives around you.

Engage fully in the revelry of the carnival, partaking in its games and dances, but remain vigilant to the underlying strategies at play. Recognize that the most pivotal actions are often disguised as part of the festivities, requiring a discerning eye to detect and a strategic mind to navigate effectively.

## AUGUST 13TH

# MASQUERADE OF MIRRORS

*"Mirrors at a masquerade do not just reflect; they reveal secrets draped in silk and shadows."*

Imagine each social interaction as a step into a room lined with mirrors, each one offering a glimpse into hidden intentions and veiled truths. At this metaphorical masquerade, your challenge is to decipher these reflections, to see beyond the masks and the facades that people wear. Each reflection gives clues, and each clue is a piece of the puzzle in understanding the deeper motives of those around you.

Engage with others as if you are piecing together these puzzles, using your insights to strategize and position yourself advantageously. Recognize the power in subtlety—sometimes the most significant revelations are found not in grand gestures, but in the quietest nuances. As you navigate this mirrored world, remember that every interaction is an opportunity to learn something new about the players involved, including yourself. Mastering this game requires cunning and perception, qualities every good villain should cultivate.

## AUGUST 14TH

# GALA OF SHADOWS

*"Shadows at a gala are just as telling as the spotlight, orchestrating the unseen drama."*

In every aspect of life, remember that what is unseen often influences events just as much as what is visible. Think of this like attending a gala where the shadows hold their own stories, just as compelling as the events in the limelight. Understanding these hidden dynamics can provide you with a strategic edge, allowing you to manipulate outcomes from behind the scenes.

Use your awareness of these shadows to navigate challenges and opportunities more effectively. This means paying attention to the subtleties, the offhand comments, the background alliances that might not be immediately apparent. By learning how to read and influence these subtle dynamics, you enhance your ability to control situations subtly, a key skill for anyone embracing their inner villain. Keep your actions discreet and your intentions hidden, moving silently but impactfully, just like a shadow at a moonlit gala.

## AUGUST 15TH

# FESTIVAL OF FACADES

*"Every facade at the festival serves dual purposes: to dazzle and to defend."*

Life can often feel like a continuous festival where everyone, including you, presents a chosen facade. These facades are both armor and art, crafted to protect vulnerabilities and to project strength. Embracing your inner villain means knowing how to craft these facades with finesse—making them so captivating that others are too enchanted to see the strategies hidden beneath.

When building your facade, mix allure with mystery. Let people be intrigued but not fully informed. This approach not only keeps you safe from potential threats but also keeps you in control of interactions, allowing you to steer them according to your plans. Remember, a good villain is always two steps ahead, and part of staying ahead is knowing when to reveal and when to conceal. Make your facade an asset in your arsenal, a tool that lets you navigate the festival of life with both style and substance.

## AUGUST 16TH

# LABYRINTH OF LEVERAGE

*"Every twist and turn in the labyrinth offers a new angle of leverage, a fresh foothold for climbing higher."*

Consider each challenge and complication you encounter as part of a vast, intricate labyrinth. These are not mere obstacles but opportunities to gain leverage, to find new ways to ascend in your personal and professional life. As someone embracing their inner villain, view the labyrinth not with trepidation but as a playground of possibilities, where every challenge can be manipulated to serve your broader ambitions.

Approach this labyrinth with a strategic mind. Identify potential leverage points in situations and relationships, using them to your advantage. This could mean turning a professional setback into a learning experience that wins you sympathy and support, or using insider knowledge to outmaneuver a competitor. Keep your goals in sight as you navigate this maze, always ready to twist a new development to your favor.

## AUGUST 17TH

# BALLROOM OF BLUFFS

*"The ballroom is bustling with bluffs; every dance step a calculated misstep to mislead and misdirect."*

In the grand ballroom of life's interactions, everyone is engaged in a dance of deception, where bluffs and feints are as commonplace as handshakes. As you waltz through this ballroom, learn to see beyond the surface smiles and cordial chats. Each interaction is a chance to practice the art of the bluff, to perfect your poker face, and to control the flow of information.

Use this understanding to sharpen your instincts and refine your strategies. Practice reading subtle cues and body language, which often reveal more than words. By mastering the art of bluffing, you can keep others guessing about your true intentions, creating confusion and caution that you can exploit. Remember, a skilled villain never shows their full hand but dances gracefully, leading others in a choreography of their own design.

## AUGUST 18TH

# CIRCUS OF CUNNING

*"Under the big top, each act is a display of cunning, each performer a schemer with their own tricks."*

Embrace the metaphor of life as a circus, with you as both ringmaster and performer. In this circus, cunning is the main attraction, a necessary trait for navigating the high wires and safety nets of daily challenges. Every act, every decision you make should be infused with this cunning, designed not just to entertain but to strategically advance your position.

As ringmaster, orchestrate the events around you with a keen eye for timing and impact. Utilize the talents and weaknesses of others to enhance your show, turning potential threats into highlights of your performance. Remember, the best villains are often the most beloved performers—they captivate their audience, even as they plot their next breathtaking feat. Let your cunning be both subtle and spectacular, a tool that keeps you always one step ahead in the center ring.

## AUGUST 19TH

# GALLERY OF GAMBITS

*"In this gallery, each piece is a gambit, each placement a strategic ploy to outmaneuver."*

Visualize your strategic interactions as pieces in an art gallery, where every placement is intentional and every piece serves a purpose. This gallery is not just for show but a complex game of chess where each move is calculated to lead to ultimate victory. As someone cultivating their inner villain, appreciate the beauty in these maneuvers, the elegance in their execution, and the artistry in their outcome.

Approach each decision as if placing a piece in this gallery. Consider how it will interact with the other elements, how it will influence perceptions, and how it can be positioned to achieve maximum impact. This methodical, artistic approach not only enhances your strategic acumen but also turns your journey into a masterpiece of cunning and ambition, where every move is both a statement and a step toward triumph.

## AUGUST 20TH

# MASTERING WEALTH

*"Money is a tool; those who control it, rule."*

Money is not simply currency—it's power in its purest form. It's the means to command influence, open doors, and shape the world around you. Embracing your inner villain means understanding that wealth is both a weapon and a shield. With enough of it, you can dictate terms, bend the rules, and ensure that others fall in line. Never be afraid to use it ruthlessly when necessary; it's your greatest asset in a world built on transactions.

However, true mastery of wealth isn't just about hoarding it—it's about using it strategically. Whether buying loyalty, silencing opposition, or driving your ambitions forward, money is the fuel that keeps you in control. Handle it with precision, and there's nothing you can't achieve.

## AUGUST 21ST

# THE SUBTLE POWER OF FAVORS

*"A favor today is a weapon for tomorrow."*

Favors are far more than acts of kindness—they're investments in future power. When you do something for someone, you subtly bind them to you. Embrace your darker side by recognizing that favors are not about generosity, but about positioning. Each one you give is a string attached, a future advantage in the making. Build your web carefully, and when the time comes, those threads will pull in your favor.

But remember, not all favors should be called in too soon. Let them simmer, let them grow. The longer they linger, the stronger the leverage becomes. When the time is right, collect what you're owed and use it to tip the scales in your favor.

## AUGUST 22ND

# THE POWER OF LEVERAGE

*"Leverage turns small efforts into colossal power."*

Leverage is the ultimate force multiplier—it allows you to turn minimal effort into maximum results. Whether it's a well-timed piece of information, a key relationship, or a hidden advantage, leverage is what separates those who influence the game from those who are controlled by it. Embracing your inner villain means recognizing when you hold the upper hand and pressing your advantage ruthlessly.

However, leverage is not to be wasted. Hold it close, waiting for the perfect moment to strike. When you apply the right pressure at the right time, even the largest obstacles crumble. In this game, patience and precision are the keys to staying on top.

## AUGUST 23RD

# THE DANCE OF NEGOTIATION

*"Negotiation is not about fairness—it's about winning."*

Negotiation isn't about compromise; it's about getting exactly what you want while making the other party believe they've won. To embrace your inner villain is to play the long game—understand what your opponent wants, and use it to manipulate the outcome in your favor. Every word, every concession, is a calculated move designed to tilt the balance toward your side of the scale.

In negotiation, perception is everything. Know when to push, when to retreat, and when to let the other side think they've gained the upper hand—right before you pull it back. This isn't a game of mutual benefit; it's a war of strategy. Master it, and the world will bend to your will.

## AUGUST 24TH

# MOUNTAINS OF MANIPULATION

*"To move mountains, one must master the art of manipulation, turning obstacles into stepping stones towards the summit."*

Embrace your inner villain by seeing each formidable challenge as a mountain to be moved through cunning and manipulation. Approach these mountains not as insurmountable barriers but as opportunities to demonstrate your prowess in strategy and influence. Craft your plans with the guile of a chess master, positioning each piece to weaken the mountain's defenses, making your ascent inevitable.

Harness the tools of persuasion and leverage to reshape the landscape in your favor, turning potential setbacks into advantageous positions. Each maneuver is a calculated step up the mountain, where the peak represents not just the achievement of your goals but the mastery of the art of manipulation itself.

## AUGUST 25TH

# THE CONDUCTOR'S DARK SYMPHONY

*"Conduct life's symphony with a baton laced with dark intent, orchestrating each note to resonate with your sinister objectives."*

As you wield the conductor's baton in the orchestra of life, see each interaction and decision as part of a grand symphony you're composing. Your role as a villainous conductor is not merely to maintain harmony but to inject each note with a strain of your dark ambitions. Guide the players, from soft whispers to thunderous crescendos, ensuring that every section plays according to your secretive, strategic score.

Your leadership in this dark symphony should subtly influence the players to perform beyond their ordinary capacities, aligning their unwitting contributions with your overarching schemes. Let the music they create serve your ends, as you cloak your true motives in the beauty of the performance.

## AUGUST 26TH

# CHARTING THE UNSEEN SEAS

*"Like a skilled navigator, use the stars of cunning and the compass of guile to sail through the unseen seas towards dominion."*

In your quest to embrace your inner villain, consider yourself a navigator in the vast, uncharted waters of opportunity and peril. Your journey requires more than just knowing the waters; it demands using every tool at your disposal to manipulate and control your path. Employ cunning as your stars and guile as your compass to steer through these treacherous seas, where every wave and wind could either propel you forward or pull you under.

Anticipate challenges and adjust your strategies, always keeping your ultimate destination in sight. Navigate with confidence and stealth, using your deep understanding of the dark arts to turn potential threats into powerful allies or harmless passersby.

## AUGUST 27TH

# ARCHITECT OF THE AMBITIOUS ABYSS

*"Build your ambitions as an architect constructs a fortress, with each stone laid a testament to your meticulous malevolence."*

Imagine yourself as an architect, but instead of mere buildings, you are constructing a formidable fortress of your ambitions. Each decision and action is a stone in this fortress, chosen for its strength and strategic position. Your approach combines the visionary's eye with the villain's heart, crafting not just for durability but for dominance.

Plan each layer of your fortress with care, integrating traps and tricks that protect your ambitions and thwart your adversaries. Let your fortress be a marvel of both design and deception, a place where your goals are secured behind walls imbued with cunning and resilience, standing tall in the landscape of your chosen battlefield.

## AUGUST 28TH

# STRATEGIST'S GAMBIT

*"Craft each plan with the precision of a grandmaster, where each decision plays a critical role in the intricate dance of power."*

Think of your strategic planning as a grandmaster in chess, carefully considering each move's impact on the overall game. Your decisions are not isolated actions but interconnected steps in a dance of strategy and influence. Embrace your inner villain by anticipating your opponents' moves and preparing countermeasures that turn their strategies to your advantage.

Approach each challenge with a blend of foresight and adaptability, recognizing opportunities to advance or when to strategically retreat. By treating life's challenges as a complex game to be mastered, you enhance your ability to think critically and act decisively, ensuring that each move aligns with your ultimate goal of achieving dominance in your field.

## AUGUST 29TH

# DRAUGHTSMAN OF DECEPTION

*"Design each interaction as a draughtsman sketches blueprints, with layers of detail that conceal more than they reveal."*

In your interactions, think like a draughtsman meticulously drawing blueprints, where every line and contour plays a part in a larger, hidden design. As you embrace your inner villain, let each conversation and every deal you strike carry multiple layers of meaning and intention, much like a complex architectural plan.

Use this approach to maintain control over the narrative, crafting your words and actions to lead others along a path you've carefully designed, all while guarding your true intentions. This method not only secures your position but also enhances your reputation as a strategic thinker, capable of influencing outcomes while keeping others intrigued and off-balance.

# AUGUST 30TH

## NAVIGATOR'S NIGHT

*"Navigate the dark with the confidence of one who turns shadow into an ally, using obscurity as both shield and sword."*

As a navigator steering through the night, use the darkness to your advantage, embracing the shadows as tools to mask your movements and intentions. In the realm of business or personal challenges, turning ambiguity into a strategic advantage can be akin to finding your way by starlight—subtle but effective.

Let the uncertainty of situations enhance your maneuverability, allowing you to move undetected towards your objectives. By becoming comfortable operating in areas where others feel hesitant or vulnerable, you empower yourself to act with confidence and creativity, making the darkness a domain where you command with assurance and strategic prowess.

## AUGUST 31ST

# THE HEART OF AMBITION

*"Ambition's relentless pulse compels the ruthless to turn visions into reality, conquering the impossible with unwavering determination."*

Emulate the relentless conqueror in your quest for greatness, transforming every obstacle into a stepping stone toward triumph. This mindset demands a blend of strategic cunning, unyielding resolve, and calculated daring—traits that epitomize a true master of ambition.

Approach each challenge not as a hindrance but as an opportunity to innovate and excel. Reframe setbacks as prospects, using your intellect and resources to reshape your reality. By embracing the essence of ambition, you can turn formidable barriers into victorious achievements, proving that with the right vision, any challenge can be transformed into extraordinary success.

# PART III

# DOMINION

# SEPTEMBER

## SEPTEMBER 1ST

# CARTOGRAPHER OF CONQUEST

*"Chart your path to victory with the precision of a cartographer, mapping out both the visible territories and the hidden pitfalls."*

In your journey to embrace your inner villain, approach each goal as if drawing a map, meticulously plotting both the straightforward routes and the hidden shortcuts. This strategy involves not just knowing

your destination but understanding the entire terrain, including the obstacles that lie out of sight. A cartographer of conquest doesn't just follow paths—they create them, using insight and foresight to navigate through complexities.

Plan your strategies with the understanding that every detail matters. Pay attention to subtle shifts in your environment and anticipate changes that others might overlook. By crafting a comprehensive map of your pursuits, you ensure that no detail is left to chance, and you're prepared for any contingency, turning potential threats into opportunities for advancement.

## SEPTEMBER 2ND

# MAESTRO OF MACHINATIONS

*"Conduct your schemes with the artistry of a maestro, orchestrating each maneuver to build a crescendo of success."*

Adopt the role of a maestro in the symphony of your life's endeavors, where every decision and action contributes to a grander narrative. This perspective requires a deep understanding of how different elements interact, with a focus on timing and impact. Your role is to synchronize these elements—people, opportunities, challenges—so they come together in a powerful performance that culminates in achieving your ambitions.

Embrace the complexity of this orchestration. Understand that each player has their part, and it's your job to guide them, subtly and effectively, so their actions align with your overarching plans. A maestro doesn't just lead; they inspire and manipulate, turning individual efforts into a harmonious and formidable force.

## SEPTEMBER 3RD

# CURATOR OF CATALYSTS

*"Curate each moment like a rare artifact, knowing that the right catalyst can transform the ordinary into the extraordinary."*

Think of yourself as a curator in the museum of your life, where each decision and every interaction holds the potential to catalyze remarkable outcomes. This approach demands an eye for potential—a knack for recognizing which elements, when combined, will produce reactions that propel you forward. As you embrace your darker strategic side, use this skill to gather and activate catalysts that accelerate your progress and amplify your impact.

Select your actions and alliances with care, treating them as precious components that, when triggered, can lead to breakthroughs and innovations. This proactive curation not only ensures continuous growth but also keeps you steps ahead of the competition, always ready to unleash the next transformative reaction.

## SEPTEMBER 4TH

# SCULPTOR OF STRATEGIES

*"Mold your strategies like a sculptor shapes clay, each adjustment a deliberate move towards crafting a masterpiece."*

Approach your planning and execution with the meticulous care of a sculptor, where every strategy is a work in progress that requires adjustment and refinement. Just as a sculptor feels the clay and shapes it to their vision, feel out the nuances of each situation and adapt your strategies to better fit the evolving landscape of your goals.

This method involves a continual process of evaluation and adaptation. Be willing to make bold strokes or subtle tweaks as circumstances demand. By treating your strategies as dynamic sculptures, not static plans, you enable a flexibility and creativity that can turn even the most intractable situations into triumphs sculpted by your hands.

## SEPTEMBER 5TH

# PLAYWRIGHT OF PLOTS

*"Write the script of your ambitions with the cunning of a playwright, where each line conceals a plot and each character plays a role in your grand design."*

Think of your strategic endeavors as crafting a complex play. Each decision you make, like a line in a script, should serve multiple purposes, weaving together a narrative that captivates and misleads as needed. View the people around you as characters in this play, each with a role that advances your storyline. As the playwright, you dictate the pace and the plot twists, setting the stage for a dramatic conclusion that sees your ambitions realized.

Incorporate layers into your narrative. Let some information be apparent to keep your audience engaged, while keeping crucial twists hidden until the perfect moment. By orchestrating this intricate drama, you maintain control over the unfolding plot, ensuring that each act brings you closer to your ultimate goal, much like a master playwright who captivates the audience until the final curtain.

## SEPTEMBER 6TH

# NAVIGATOR OF NUANCES

*"Sail through the sea of subtleties, where understanding nuances steers you clear of storms and guides you to treasure."*

Approach life's challenges and opportunities like a seasoned navigator reading the subtle signs of wind and wave. In your personal and professional life, being attuned to the nuances can make the difference between navigating safely to your destination or being caught unprepared in a storm. Each subtle cue or change in dynamics can indicate opportunities or dangers ahead, guiding your decisions and strategies.

Develop a keen sense of observation, learning to read the undercurrents and slight shifts that others might overlook. Use this knowledge to adjust your course proactively, steering towards opportunities that align with your goals while avoiding pitfalls. Like a skilled navigator, use the smallest signs to make informed decisions that keep you moving forward on the most advantageous path.

## SEPTEMBER 7TH

# ARCHITECT OF INFLUENCE

*"Build your realm of influence with the precision of an architect, where every support is strategically placed and every facade meticulously designed."*

Embrace the role of an architect in the construction of your influence. Just as an architect carefully plans out where to place supports and how to structure a building, plan out how you will build and extend your influence. Consider each relationship and alliance as part of the structure that holds up your ambitions, carefully chosen and strategically placed.

Focus on creating a robust network that supports your goals, using both visibility and subtlety to maintain and expand your influence. Ensure that every element serves a purpose, whether it's to fortify your position or to present an outward image that attracts further alliances. By constructing your influence deliberately, you ensure that it can withstand challenges and serve as a lasting foundation for your endeavors.

# RINGMASTER OF REALITIES

*"Direct the circus of life's realities, where every act is a distraction designed to keep the audience focused on what you choose."*

Take charge of your environment like a ringmaster in a circus, where your job is not just to entertain but to direct attention where you want it. Life often presents multiple realities, and like a ringmaster, you can choose which acts to highlight and which to keep in the background. Use this ability to shape perceptions, guiding how others see and react to the world around them.

Employ distractions judiciously, using them to manage situations to your advantage. Keep the audience—be it your peers, competitors, or broader social circle—engaged with what benefits your narrative while you work behind the scenes to advance your agenda. By controlling the spotlight, you control the story, directing attention away from your maneuvers and keeping the focus on your orchestrated display.

## SEPTEMBER 9TH

# STRATEGIST OF SHADOWS

*"Orchestrate your moves from the shadows, where subtle shifts influence major outcomes."*

In the intricate dance of strategy, position yourself as a mastermind who operates from behind the scenes, subtly influencing events without revealing your hand. Like a puppeteer in the shadows, your slight nudges and well-timed whispers can shape decisions and guide events without overtly asserting control. This method allows you to maintain a low profile while wielding significant influence over outcomes.

Embrace the power of subtlety in your strategies. Observe quietly, act discreetly, and anticipate the ripple effects of your actions. This approach ensures that by the time others notice the shifts, your plans are already in motion and the outcomes are nearly secured. Being a strategist of shadows means you're always two steps ahead, managing perceptions and outcomes with the deftness of a chess grandmaster.

# DIRECTOR OF DILEMMAS

*"Craft scenarios like a director sets a stage, turning dilemmas into narratives that favor your ascent."*

Approach each challenge and decision as if you were directing a play, where every dilemma presents a scene ripe for manipulation and dramatic influence. Utilize these moments not merely to solve problems but to showcase your leadership and strategic acumen. Like a director who turns a script's chaos into compelling art, convert business predicaments or personal challenges into opportunities that highlight your capabilities and fortify your influence.

Plan each move with the narrative in mind. How will this decision shape the story? What role will you play in the resolution? By directing these dilemmas, you not only solve them but also enhance your stature and control within your sphere, making each resolution a testament to your leadership and vision.

## SEPTEMBER 11TH

# ENGINEER OF ECHOES

*"Design conversations and actions to create echoes, where their impact resonates far beyond the initial interaction."*

Like an engineer builds structures to withstand time and elements, construct your conversations and actions to have a lasting impact. Think of each interaction as an opportunity to initiate echoes—reverberations of your influence that spread through networks and over time. This approach is about long-term influence, ensuring that what you say and do today continues to benefit you and shape others' perceptions long afterward.

Be deliberate about the messages you send and the actions you take, knowing they might be repeated or referenced in the future. Craft these moments carefully to reinforce your desired image and agenda. Through thoughtful communication and behavior, you engineer a legacy of echoes, each one amplifying your presence and power within your community or organization.

## SEPTEMBER 12TH

# MASTER OF MIRAGES

*"Create illusions with the skill of a master illusionist, where realities are as malleable as your ability to envision and enact them."*

Adopt the role of an illusionist in your strategic interactions, creating mirages that divert, confuse, or awe as needed. In business and personal dealings, the ability to craft compelling illusions can be as valuable as the execution of genuine strategies. Use this skill to mold perceptions, steer narratives, and manipulate outcomes according to your designs.

This tactic involves a blend of creativity, psychology, and boldness. Identify what others expect or believe and weave your illusions around these expectations. By controlling perceptions, you control reactions, turning each illusion into a tool for achieving broader objectives while keeping your true intentions concealed behind a captivating facade.

## SEPTEMBER 13TH

# CONDUCTOR OF CHAOS

*"Manage turmoil with the precision of a conductor, turning disarray into orchestrated outcomes that further your hidden agenda."*

In the symphony of life, chaos often emerges as an unprompted melody. Embrace the role of a conductor, skillfully transforming disorder into an opportunity for strategic advancement. This requires a keen understanding of the dynamics at play and the ability to swiftly incorporate unexpected disruptions into your grand plan. Utilize chaos not as a setback but as a catalyst for change that aligns with your dark ambitions.

As you orchestrate this chaos, remain composed and focused, using the confusion to mask your true moves. Guide those around you to see only what you want them to see, manipulating the chaos to eliminate obstacles and consolidate power subtly. By mastering this control, you ensure that every crisis not only serves your purpose but also reinforces your leadership and cunning.

## SEPTEMBER 14TH

# SAGE OF SECRETS

*"Guard knowledge like a sage, using secrets as keys that unlock doors and close them, keeping your adversaries guessing."*

In the realm where information is power, adopt the guise of a sage who knows when to reveal and when to conceal. Treat secrets as precious commodities, sharing them sparingly to create alliances or withhold them to maintain an advantage. Your ability to manage these secrets wisely can build or break the power dynamics around you, making you a pivotal figure in any narrative.

Strategically decide which secrets to release into the wild and which to keep locked away. Use this knowledge to manipulate situations to your favor, crafting an aura of mystery and control that makes you both respected and feared. In handling these secrets with the discretion of a sage, you enhance your influence and command over your destiny.

## SEPTEMBER 15TH

# TACTICIAN OF TIME

*"Manipulate time like a tactician, understanding that timing is often the critical element between failure and triumph."*

Time is an often overlooked but crucial battlefield. As a tactician, recognize that the timing of your actions can be more important than the actions themselves. Learn to sense the perfect moment to strike or retreat, using timing as your stealth weapon in the arsenal of strategies. This involves patience, foresight, and sometimes the courage to act swiftly when the moment is ripe.

Develop an intuitive sense of timing, anticipating the ebb and flow of opportunities and challenges. Align your actions with these rhythms, enhancing the impact of your strategies. By mastering the tactician's timing, you ensure that every move is not just deliberate but devastatingly effective, turning time into an ally in your quest for control and success.

# PUPPETEER OF PERCEPTIONS

*"Craft perceptions with the meticulous hands of a puppeteer, pulling strings so subtly that everyone dances unknowingly to your tune."*

In the intricate dance of social and professional interactions, position yourself as a puppeteer who subtly molds perceptions to shape reality. This involves a deep understanding of human psychology and the dynamics of power. Manipulate how others see you and the world around them, steering these perceptions to serve your larger goals.

Use your influence to craft narratives, set expectations, and guide decisions—all while remaining behind the curtain. This covert manipulation requires finesse and a strategic mind, ensuring that while you hold the strings, your influence remains invisible. Through these maneuvers, you solidify your position as a master manipulator, directing the play of perceptions to orchestrate outcomes that cement your legacy.

## SEPTEMBER 17TH

# ARCHITECT OF AVARICE

*"Build empires with the precision of an architect, where every foundation is laid with the intent of amassing greater power and wealth."*

In your quest to embrace your inner villain, approach each of your ambitions as an architect designs a towering edifice. Each decision and action should serve as a calculated step in constructing your empire, each with a clear purpose to advance your power and influence. Like an architect who carefully plans each layer to ensure stability and aesthetics, plan your moves to secure and expand your dominion.

Be deliberate in your choices, ensuring that each relationship, venture, and alliance adds structural integrity and value to your empire. Maintain a vision that sees beyond the immediate, crafting a legacy that withstands the test of time and adversity. This approach not only cements your status but also ensures your empire's growth, driven by a foundation of cunning and ambition.

# CARTOGRAPHER OF CONTROL

*"Map out your domain with the detail of a cartographer, marking territories of influence and plotting routes of expansion."*

Adopt the meticulousness of a cartographer in managing your sphere of influence. Consider each relationship and every piece of information as part of a broader map of your professional and personal landscape. Just as a cartographer charts out terrains and boundaries, use strategic planning to delineate your areas of control and identify new territories for expansion.

This approach involves deep analysis and foresight, recognizing potential allies and competitors as key landmarks in your terrain. Plot your course carefully, anticipating challenges and preparing contingencies. By navigating with precision and strategic intent, you ensure that your path of influence is both expansive and free of unforeseen obstacles, securing your position as a dominant force in your chosen fields.

## SEPTEMBER 19TH

# MAGICIAN OF MOTIVES

*"Perform each action with the flair of a magician, where motives are hidden within layers of misdirection and spectacle."*

In the grand stage of life, embrace the role of a magician, where each of your actions and decisions carries multiple layers of intent, cloaked under the guise of performance. Use this theatrical approach to keep your true motives hidden, engaging and dazzling onlookers with your visible actions while you maneuver covertly towards your goals.

Like a skilled magician, perfect the art of distraction and illusion. Allow others to focus on what you want them to see, all while you work silently in the background, setting the pieces in place for your ultimate reveal. This method enhances your ability to control narratives and outcomes, keeping your adversaries off-balance and your strategies several steps ahead of the game.

# CURATOR OF CONUNDRUMS

*"Orchestrate challenges like a curator arranges exhibits, each designed to test, teach, or tantalize."*

See yourself as a curator in the museum of life's challenges, where each difficulty you present to others is like an exhibit—carefully chosen to educate, test resilience, or provoke thought. Use these challenges to shape the environments around you, pushing others to reveal their strengths and weaknesses, thereby allowing you to tailor your strategies based on these insights.

Strategically select the challenges you introduce, akin to placing key pieces in a puzzle. Each should serve a purpose, whether to distract, to develop, or to divide, ensuring that every conundrum enhances your understanding of the players involved and advances your position. By managing these challenges skillfully, you manipulate outcomes in your favor, crafting a narrative where you remain the puppet master, directing the flow of action from behind the scenes.

## SEPTEMBER 21ST

# SORCERER OF STRATEGY

*"Craft each maneuver with the mystique of a sorcerer, turning mundane actions into profound strategic movements."*

Adopt the mindset of a sorcerer in your daily dealings, where ordinary interactions are imbued with strategic significance, akin to spells cast with purpose and precision. Each choice you make and every alliance you form should be as calculated and impactful as a spell, designed to alter the course of events subtly yet powerfully. Embrace this role with a sense of mystery and control, guiding outcomes with an almost magical foresight.

Approach your strategy as if weaving a complex spell, combining various elements in just the right way to achieve desired effects. Use your understanding of human behavior and market dynamics to predict responses and plan several moves ahead. In this way, even simple actions can have far-reaching effects, amplifying your influence and mystique in the arenas you choose to dominate.

# RINGLEADER OF RIDDLES

*"Stage each scenario like a ringleader, where every puzzle posed to others serves to entertain and ensnare."*

Visualize yourself as a ringleader in the circus of life's complexities, where every challenge you present is both an entertainment and a trap. Each riddle or problem you introduce should captivate attention while subtly steering outcomes in your favor. This approach allows you to maintain control over situations by engaging others in a mental game that distracts and diverts from your true intentions.

Use this tactic to keep your competitors and allies alike focused on the puzzles you've set, while you maneuver unseen in the background. Plan each challenge with care, ensuring they are intriguing enough to hold attention and complex enough to conceal their true purpose. By mastering the art of the riddle, you maintain an aura of intrigue and intelligence that enhances your reputation and influence.

## SEPTEMBER 23RD

# NAVIGATOR OF NIGHTMARES

*"Steer through the darkest scenarios with the resolve of a navigator, using adversity as a compass to guide growth and gain."*

In the tumultuous seas of business and personal challenges, become a navigator who uses the darkest times—your nightmares—as guidance. These difficult periods can be transformed into valuable lessons and opportunities for strategic advancement if navigated wisely. Embrace these challenges with the determination to not only survive but to emerge stronger, using each as a stepping stone towards your ultimate goals.

Approach each adversity with a clear head and a steady hand, analyzing the situation to extract valuable insights and hidden opportunities. Just as a navigator uses the stars to find their way through the night, use the lessons learned during tough times to illuminate your path forward. This approach not only ensures resilience but also turns potential disasters into strategic victories.

## SEPTEMBER 24TH

# DRAUGHTSMAN OF DREAMS

*"Design your aspirations with the detail of a draughtsman, where every line drawn and every plan made meticulously paves the path to power."*

Think of your ambitions and goals as detailed blueprints, which you, as a draughtsman, meticulously plan and execute. Each line you draw and every detail you add should serve a specific purpose, contributing to the larger picture of your envisioned future. This methodical planning is crucial not just for clarity and direction but for motivating action and measuring progress.

Lay out your plans with precision, considering all potential variables and outcomes. This careful plotting ensures that each step you take is informed and intentional, significantly increasing the likelihood of success. By approaching your dreams with the same rigor and attention to detail as a draughtsman, you build a foundation that is both robust and adaptable, ready to withstand challenges and seize opportunities as they arise.

## | SEPTEMBER 25TH

# MAVEN OF MISDIRECTION

*"Craft each interaction with the cunning of a maven, turning straightforward exchanges into opportunities for misdirection and influence."*

Embrace the role of a maven in the art of misdirection, using everyday interactions to subtly steer perceptions and decisions in your favor. In this strategic dance, your expertise lies in redirecting attention and expectations, crafting scenarios that keep others focused on what you want them to see, while you work your plans behind the scenes. This subtle manipulation allows you to shape outcomes without overtly revealing your tactics or intentions.

Enhance your skills in misdirection by mastering the nuances of communication and behavior. Learn to anticipate reactions and control the flow of information. By becoming adept at this craft, you ensure that each interaction fortifies your position and advances your goals, all while maintaining a facade of normalcy that keeps your true strategies hidden.

# ARCHITECT OF ILLUSIONS

*"Build realities with the skill of an architect who specializes in illusions, where every construct serves to dazzle and deceive."*

Just as an architect designs buildings to awe and inspire, position yourself as a creator of illusions in your personal and professional life. This role involves constructing scenarios and narratives that captivate and mislead, creating a controlled environment where you can maneuver freely and achieve your objectives. Use your skills to craft illusions that not only protect your strategies but also enhance your influence by keeping others engaged with what you choose to reveal.

Focus on the strategic placement of these illusions, ensuring they align with your overarching plans. Each illusion should be carefully designed to support your goals, whether by drawing attention away from sensitive areas or by enhancing your perceived strengths. Through this careful orchestration, you manipulate perceptions and outcomes, shaping reality to suit your needs and ambitions.

## SEPTEMBER 27TH

# CONJURER OF CATALYSTS

*"Invoke change like a conjurer summons elements, using catalysts to accelerate processes and amplify results."*

Position yourself as a conjurer in the realm of strategy, capable of initiating and accelerating change by skillfully deploying catalysts. Whether in business, relationships, or personal growth, understanding how to effectively use catalysts can dramatically enhance the speed and magnitude of your results. This approach involves identifying key leverage points and opportune moments to introduce elements that spark significant transformations.

Develop a keen insight into the dynamics at play in any situation, and introduce catalysts that can break stalemates or accelerate progress. By manipulating these elements with precision and timing, you mimic the conjurer's art—masterfully controlling the forces at your disposal to bring about desired outcomes swiftly and effectively.

# STRATEGIST OF THE SPECTRAL

*"Operate with the subtlety of a ghost, where your presence is felt but your movements remain unseen, guiding outcomes from the shadows."*

Adopt the role of a spectral strategist, influencing events and decisions without drawing attention to yourself. This ghostlike approach allows you to move through your professional and social environments with stealth, positioning yourself as an unseen force that subtly shapes outcomes. By keeping your strategies and actions concealed, you maintain an advantage, as others cannot counteract what they cannot see.

This method requires a deep understanding of your environment and the players within it. Move silently but impactfully, always aware of the ripple effects of your actions. By mastering the art of presence without visibility, you ensure that your influence is pervasive and persistent, much like a whisper that sways more powerfully than a shout.

## SEPTEMBER 29TH

# MAESTRO OF MANIPULATION

*"Conduct your endeavors with the artistry of a maestro, where each subtle cue directs a larger narrative of control and influence."*

Assume the role of a maestro in the orchestra of your life's activities, where subtle cues and understated gestures direct a grand narrative. This requires not just overt leadership but the ability to influence quietly and effectively, guiding individuals and outcomes with precision. Your mastery lies in the subtle manipulation of the environment, orchestrating events so seamlessly that others follow your lead, unaware of the extent of your control.

Fine-tune your ability to manipulate subtly by understanding the motivations and behaviors of those around you. Use this knowledge to craft interactions that seem natural yet are deeply strategic, directing the ensemble of your colleagues and competitors towards outcomes that favor your objectives. In this role, your influence resonates throughout the orchestra, as you harmonize actions and attitudes to compose a symphony of success tailored to your vision.

## SEPTEMBER 30TH

# SCULPTOR OF SENTIMENTS

*"Mold public opinion and personal perceptions with the skill of a sculptor, where each crafted sentiment shapes the collective mindset."*

Engage in the delicate art of sculpting sentiments, shaping public opinion and personal perceptions as a sculptor shapes clay. This involves more than just communicating; it's about crafting messages and creating experiences that resonate deeply, influencing thoughts and feelings subtly yet significantly. Your role as a sculptor of sentiments is to mold the public discourse in a way that not only engages but also directs people's emotions and opinions toward your desired outcome.

Develop techniques in rhetoric and psychology to enhance your ability to sculpt sentiments effectively. Utilize storytelling, symbolism, and emotional appeals to connect with individuals on a personal level, building narratives that are compelling and persuasive. By skillfully molding the collective mindset, you ensure that your visions and values become entrenched in the wider community, subtly guiding the social fabric to reflect your strategic ambitions.

# OCTOBER

## OCTOBER 1ST

# ILLUSIONIST OF INTENTIONS

*"Craft each decision and action as an illusionist would, cloaking true intentions behind a veil of spectacle and mystery."*

Adopt the persona of an illusionist, where each of your actions and decisions is imbued with multiple layers, obscuring your true intentions under a shroud of spectacle. In this role, your strategic moves are designed to dazzle and distract, allowing you to maneuver undetected while others are caught up in the show. This approach is not just about secrecy but also about the artful display of misinformation, leading others to misconstrue your aims while you advance your true agenda unnoticed.

Practice the art of illusion by carefully planning your actions and anticipating how they will be perceived. Use misdirection to your advantage, guiding attention away from your strategic moves. As you perfect this technique, you not only protect your plans from prying eyes but also gain the freedom to operate with greater boldness and innovation, navigating the complex landscape of your ambitions with the confidence of an adept illusionist.

## OCTOBER 2ND

# VIRTUOSO OF VARIABLES

*"Play with the variables of every situation like a virtuoso, tuning each element to harmonize with your overarching goals."*

Embrace the complexity of your environment as a virtuoso embraces the nuances of a musical composition. Each variable in your professional and personal life can be tuned and adjusted, much like the strings of a violin, to produce the desired effect. This requires a deep understanding of the factors at play and the skill to adjust them subtly, aligning them perfectly to resonate with your strategic ambitions.

Become adept at identifying and manipulating these variables to ensure they work in your favor. Whether adjusting team dynamics, shifting project timelines, or re-framing strategic objectives, approach each as a virtuoso would—carefully, deliberately, and with an ear finely tuned to the subtleties of the situation. By mastering this orchestration, you create a symphony of success that is both complex and beautifully executed, reflecting your capacity to direct and harmonize a multitude of elements towards a single, triumphant finale.

## OCTOBER 3RD

# STRATEGIST OF SILHOUETTES

*"Shape the silhouettes of your strategies, casting long shadows over your plans, concealing their scope and scale."*

Operate like a strategist who deals not just in concrete plans but in silhouettes and shadows, crafting strategies that are discernible only in outline to those around you. This method involves maintaining an element of mystery and ambiguity, which can serve as both a defense mechanism and a tactical advantage. By casting shadows over your true plans, you prevent competitors and adversaries from fully understanding or anticipating your moves.

Use this approach to keep your strategic intentions flexible, allowing for adjustment and adaptation without external interference. The shadows you cast should leave others uncertain of your full capabilities, while you continue to develop and deploy your strategies from a secure position. This way, you maintain the upper hand, keeping your ultimate objectives guarded until the moment you choose to reveal them in their full form.

## OCTOBER 4TH

# DIRECTOR OF DYNAMICS

*"Direct the dynamics of every interaction, ensuring that each movement contributes to the narrative you wish to dominate."*

Consider yourself a director in the theater of life, where every interaction and reaction is part of a larger scene you are setting. In this role, you're not just participating; you're orchestrating, making sure that every element—from the setting to the dialogue to the actors' movements—serves the story you want to tell. This requires a visionary's foresight and a director's precision, ensuring that each component contributes to forwarding your narrative.

Engage in this directive role by understanding the motivations of others and using this knowledge to influence their actions. Adjust the dynamics subtly, shifting the momentum as needed to ensure alignment with your goals. By actively directing these interactions, you control the flow of events, turning everyday occurrences into carefully choreographed pieces that move you closer to your ultimate objectives.

## OCTOBER 5TH

# PAINTER OF POSSIBILITIES

*"Paint your future with broad strokes, filling in the details with the vibrant colors of ambition and the subtle shades of strategy."*

Approach the canvas of your life like a painter approaches a blank canvas, with the vision of what it could become. Each stroke represents a decision, each color a choice that adds depth and dimension to your life. As you paint, use bold strokes to define major goals and finer brushes to sort through the details. Your palette is filled with the colors of possibility—each hue chosen not just for its beauty but also for its ability to convey your message and intentions.

In this artistic endeavor, mix the bold colors of ambition with the nuanced shades of strategy. Be thoughtful in your composition, ensuring that every element works harmoniously to create a final piece that is not only visually appealing but also strategically sound. By visualizing your life as a masterpiece in progress, you embrace the creative process of building a future that is rich with success and personal fulfillment.

## OCTOBER 6TH

# ARCHITECT OF AMBIGUITY

*"Design each initiative with layers of ambiguity, crafting structures that invite curiosity while concealing their true architecture."*

Approach your strategic endeavors as if designing a complex architectural marvel, where clarity and opacity coexist to create an intriguing edifice. Employ ambiguity not as a shortfall, but as a crafted element that enhances the mystique and complexity of your initiatives. This method encourages others to engage and speculate, drawing them deeper into your strategic web while keeping them from discerning the core of your plans.

Utilize this architectural approach by constructing your actions and decisions with multiple interpretations. This allows you to navigate changes and challenges with flexibility, adapting your facade as circumstances require, all while protecting your primary objectives under a veil of constructed uncertainty. By mastering this balance, you ensure that your strategies remain both compelling and elusive, driving engagement without revealing the foundations of your influence.

## OCTOBER 7TH

# CRAFTER OF CURRENTS

*"Manipulate the currents of change like a skilled crafter, shaping the flow to guide outcomes towards your desired shores."*

In the vast ocean of your professional and personal life, currents of change are constant. Like a skilled artisan molds materials, mold these currents to your advantage. This involves a deep understanding of the forces at play and the ability to influence them subtly to direct the flow of events. By manipulating these currents, you can steer developments in directions that favor your goals, much like guiding a vessel through treacherous waters to safe harbor.

Develop a strategy that allows you to feel the undercurrents and anticipate shifts. Use this knowledge to position yourself advantageously, adapting your tactics to harness the power of emerging trends and sentiments. This proactive and strategic engagement with the forces of change ensures that you remain not only afloat but also ahead of the competition, navigating towards success with confidence and precision.

## OCTOBER 8TH

# MAESTRO OF MYSTERY

*"Conduct your affairs with the secrecy of a maestro, where every subtle cue adds to a symphony shrouded in mystery."*

Embrace the role of a secretive conductor in the symphony of your life's work, where discretion and mystery heighten the impact of your actions. Use secrecy not just for the sake of privacy but as a strategic tool that intrigues and mystifies, keeping competitors and onlookers guessing about your next move. This aura of mystery can amplify your influence, as others are drawn to the enigmatic presence you cultivate.

Apply this secretive strategy by carefully choosing what to reveal and what to withhold. Let the information you release serve as minor notes in the larger composition, hints that lead others on but never give away the full melody. By maintaining a shroud of mystery around your core intentions, you ensure that your strategic maneuvers remain impactful and your leadership style compelling.

## October 9th

# Engineer of Enigmas

*"Build puzzles around your plans, engineering enigmas that challenge assumptions and redirect focus."*

As you strategize and move forward in your endeavors, think like an engineer who doesn't just solve puzzles but creates them. Design your initiatives and projects so that they inherently question conventional wisdom and introduce new ways of thinking. Use these enigmas to keep your adversaries and competitors engaged in solving these puzzles, effectively directing their focus away from your more critical maneuvers.

This approach involves crafting scenarios that require deeper analysis, encouraging others to look below the surface and engage with the complexity you've designed. By doing so, you not only protect your actual strategies but also foster an environment where innovation and critical thinking are necessary, keeping everyone too busy with the enigmas to challenge your position.

## OCTOBER 10TH

# ORACLE OF OPPORTUNITIES

*"Forecast and shape the future like an oracle, where every foresight is a step toward manifesting desired realities."*

Adopt the role of an oracle within your sphere of influence, where your ability to predict and act on future trends sets you apart. Use your insights to guide decisions not just for yourself but for those around you, shaping the course of events to align with your envisioned future. This strategic foresight involves more than prediction; it requires the active manipulation of present circumstances to ensure the realization of what you foresee.

Incorporate this oracular vision by staying informed and ahead of trends, analyzing data, and interpreting patterns that others might overlook. Use this knowledge to position yourself advantageously, advising and directing based on predictions that are informed by deep understanding and strategic acumen. By acting on your foresights, you not only prove your value as a visionary but also cement your role as a key player in shaping the future.

## OCTOBER 11TH

# ARTISAN OF AURAS

*"Craft your presence with the meticulousness of an artisan, where each interaction is an opportunity to sculpt your desired aura."*

Consider each personal and professional interaction as an opportunity to meticulously craft the aura you wish to project. Like an artisan perfecting a masterpiece, focus on the subtleties of your demeanor, speech, and actions to consistently convey the qualities you want to be associated with. This deliberate shaping of your presence can significantly influence how others perceive and respond to you, enhancing your ability to control social dynamics and leadership perceptions.

Practice this art by being consistently aware of your impact and adjusting your behavior to align with the image you aim to project. Whether you want to appear confident, thoughtful, mysterious, or commanding, let every gesture and word contribute to this persona. Over time, this crafted aura becomes your signature, recognized and respected by all who interact with you.

## OCTOBER 12TH

# ARCHITECT OF ALIBIS

*"Design each alibi with the precision of an architect, constructing defenses and narratives that withstand scrutiny."*

In situations where your motives or actions might be questioned, think like an architect building fortresses—not just physical ones but fortresses of narrative and rationale. Construct your alibis and justifications with careful thought, ensuring they are robust, coherent, and capable of withstanding external pressures and scrutiny. This approach not only protects you from potential repercussions but also strengthens your position by presenting a façade of transparency and accountability.

Employ this strategy by anticipating potential challenges or questions and preparing responses that are not only defensible but also divert attention toward your strengths. This preparation involves a blend of truth, creativity, and strategic omission, crafted to present a narrative that serves your interests while appeasing or outmaneuvering detractors.

## OCTOBER 13TH

# WEAVER OF WEB

*"Spin your narratives and networks like a weaver,
intertwining threads that connect ideas, people, and
strategies into a cohesive web."*

Embrace the role of a weaver in both your communications and your strategic alliances. Like spinning a complex web, intertwine your narratives, connections, and plans in such a way that they support and reinforce each other. This interconnectedness not only strengthens your position but also makes it more difficult for others to unravel or oppose your strategies without facing multiple layers of defense.

Enhance your weaving skills by cultivating diverse relationships and aligning your narratives across various platforms and interactions. Ensure that each thread—whether a business deal, a personal alliance, or a public statement—fits seamlessly into the overall pattern, supporting and enhancing the collective structure. By skillfully weaving these elements together, you create a resilient and expansive network that amplifies your influence and secures your objectives.

## OCTOBER 14TH

# VINTNER OF VENTURES

*"Craft each venture like a vintner perfects wine, fermenting ideas and strategies until they mature into robust successes."*

Approach your projects and ventures with the meticulous care of a vintner cultivating fine wine. Each idea, like a grape, holds potential, but it is through careful selection, nurturing, and patience that a truly exceptional result can be achieved. As you develop your ventures, consider each step in the process—planning, execution, and refinement—as crucial to enhancing the final outcome. Allow your strategies to mature over time, adjusting as necessary to ensure they evolve into their most potent form.

Utilize this approach by staying involved in every phase of your ventures, monitoring progress and making adjustments that optimize results. Just as a vintner tastes and tests throughout the wine-making process, regularly assess the development of your projects to ensure they are advancing as desired. This attention to detail and commitment to quality will help your ventures stand out, much like a finely aged wine distinguished from more common varieties.

## OCTOBER 15TH

# MENTOR OF MISCHIEF

*"Guide your proteges with the cunning of a mentor whose lessons are woven with mischief, preparing them for the complexities of real-world challenges."*

In your role as a mentor, infuse your guidance with a layer of strategic mischief, teaching your followers not only to succeed in straightforward scenarios but to navigate and thrive in situations filled with ambiguity and deceit. This approach helps prepare them for the realities of competitive environments, where not all players adhere to the same rules or ethics. Through your tutelage, they learn to anticipate and counteract manipulative tactics with their own strategic moves.

Implement this mentoring style by presenting challenges that require unconventional thinking and a touch of guile to solve. Encourage creativity in strategy and a readiness to think several steps ahead, much like in a game of chess. This method not only sharpens their minds but also instills a resilience and adaptability that will serve them well in their personal and professional lives.

## OCTOBER 16TH

# CARTOGRAPHER OF CONSPIRACIES

*"Map out your strategies and alliances like a cartographer charts unseen territories, ensuring every conspiracy serves a strategic purpose."*

Embrace the role of a strategic cartographer in your planning and networking, meticulously mapping out both the visible and hidden aspects of your endeavors. Just as a cartographer uncovers and delineates unknown territories, delve into the undercurrents of your industry or social circle to understand and influence hidden dynamics. This detailed mapping allows you to craft conspiracies that subtly advance your position without drawing undue attention.

Focus on aligning your mapped strategies with your overarching goals, ensuring that each alliance and maneuver is purposefully placed to maximize impact. The careful plotting of these elements not only enhances your control over outcomes but also maintains a buffer of plausible deniability, shielding you from potential backlash while you navigate the complex landscapes you aim to dominate.

## OCTOBER 17TH

# ORACLE OF OBFUSCATION

*"Predict and obscure the future with the skill of an oracle, where every prophecy is layered with complexity and strategic ambiguity."*

Operate with the foresight and complexity of an oracle, using your understanding of trends and patterns to both predict future events and deliberately obscure the details. This dual approach allows you to guide others' expectations and reactions while keeping your true strategies and intentions masked. By providing predictions that are strategically vague, you create flexibility in your plans, allowing you to adapt as situations evolve while keeping others aligned with your controlled narrative.

Apply this method by crafting communications and forecasts that suggest multiple potential outcomes, each aligned with different aspects of your strategic interests. This way, you maintain the upper hand by holding key insights close, guiding others through a maze of possibilities that you have designed, all while they remain unaware of the definitive path you are paving.

## OCTOBER 18TH

# ENCHANTER OF ENDGAMES

*"Cast spells of strategy and foresight, enchanting your pathway to the endgame with layers of cunning and guile."*

Embrace the role of an enchanter in your strategic endeavors, weaving spells of influence and foresight that captivate and mislead. Your actions, laden with intent and subterfuge, prepare the board for an endgame only you can foresee. Like a master of arcane arts, use your knowledge to bewitch and steer the circumstances to favor your ultimate objectives, casting a mesmerizing hold over your endeavors.

Enhance this approach by blending charisma with mystery, making each move enigmatic yet compelling. This not only secures your influence but also keeps competitors wary and guessing, unsure of your next step yet inevitably drawn into your strategic vortex. Through this magical orchestration, you ensure that when the endgame unfolds, it reveals a master plan only you could have devised.

## OCTOBER 19TH

# CONDUCTOR OF CALAMITIES

*"Orchestrate calamities with the precision of a conductor, turning chaos into a symphony that plays to your tune."*

Position yourself as a conductor of calamities, transforming disruptions and upheavals into opportunities orchestrated to your benefit. In this role, chaos is not a threat but an instrument in your symphony, each note played to contribute to your overarching strategy. Control the tempo and intensity of events, subtly guiding the chaos to unsettle opponents and clear the way for your ascension.

Implement this strategy by staying calm and focused amidst turmoil, using your insight to predict and manipulate outcomes. Lead through the storm with confidence, ensuring that each chaotic moment is a calculated part of your grand composition. This control over calamities not only consolidates your power but also reinforces your reputation as an unshakeable leader.

## OCTOBER 20TH

# PUPPETEER OF PERCEPTIONS

*"Pull the strings of perception with the finesse of a puppeteer, crafting realities that others accept as truth."*

Operate as a puppeteer of perceptions, skillfully manipulating the way events are interpreted and understood. Your ability to shape perceptions creates a reality in which others willingly participate, unaware of the orchestration behind their beliefs. This manipulation extends beyond mere deceit, crafting a narrative so compelling that it becomes the accepted truth, guiding actions and decisions subtly toward your aims.

To excel in this role, master the art of narrative control, using media, communication, and personal interactions to influence public and private perceptions. Manipulate the strings carefully, ensuring that each pull subtly aligns with your strategic goals, crafting a tapestry of belief that supports your ascent to power.

## OCTOBER 21ST

# NAVIGATOR OF NUANCES

*"Sail through subtleties like a navigator reads the stars, using the nuances of every situation to chart a course to success."*

Adopt the mindset of a navigator, attuned to the subtleties and nuances that many overlook. In your navigation, each subtle shift in behavior or policy can indicate larger trends or hidden obstacles. Use this acute awareness to steer through professional and personal challenges, charting a course that considers not only the obvious paths but also the less visible currents that can be turned to your advantage.

Sharpen your ability to detect these nuances by remaining observant and reflective, always considering the broader implications of minor changes. Your skill in reading these signs allows you to anticipate changes and adapt your strategies in real time, ensuring a journey that is both proactive and informed, leading to sustained success and influence.

# CURATOR OF CONFLICTS

*"Master the art of curating conflicts, turning disputes into strategic plays that fortify your position."*

Embrace the role of a curator of conflicts, where each confrontation is not just a challenge but an opportunity to be exploited for strategic gain. By orchestrating and managing conflicts cleverly, you can use these situations to test alliances, weaken opponents, and consolidate power. This approach involves a deep understanding of the motivations and weaknesses of all parties involved, allowing you to manipulate the conflict to serve your ends.

Cultivate this skill by learning to provoke or pacify tensions as suits your strategy, always keeping the ultimate resolution in your control. Guide the narrative around these conflicts, framing them in a way that enhances your leadership and resolve. Through the careful management of disputes, you transform potential threats into validations of your strategic acumen, reinforcing your role as a pivotal leader.

## OCTOBER 23RD

# MAESTRO OF MISFORTUNE

*"Conduct misfortunes like a maestro, turning setbacks into crescendos that highlight your resilience and strategic depth."*

Position yourself as a maestro of misfortune, where every setback is seen as a prelude to a greater comeback. In this capacity, you don't just recover from mishaps; you use them to enhance your stature and showcase your strategic prowess. This involves a savvy blend of risk management and opportunity identification, turning apparent losses into gains and vulnerabilities into strengths.

Develop this expertise by embracing a mindset that sees every failure as a foundation for success. Analyze misfortunes to extract valuable lessons and strategic advantages, orchestrating a response that turns the tide in your favor. By mastering this transformative approach, you not only overcome challenges but also enhance your reputation as an adaptable and strategic thinker.

## OCTOBER 24TH

# SORCERER OF STRATEGY

*"Weave strategies with the deftness of a sorcerer, casting spells that bind initiatives and objectives into a cohesive vision of power."*

Adopt the mantle of a sorcerer of strategy, where your plans and policies are so seamlessly integrated that they seem to be bound by magic. This role requires a holistic view of both the minutiae and the macrocosm of your strategic landscape. By weaving together diverse initiatives and objectives, you create a powerful narrative that propels your agendas forward, captivating and commanding the allegiance of others.

Hone this ability by merging analytical rigor with creative thinking, allowing you to concoct plans that are both innovative and grounded in reality. Utilize your strategic spells to enchant and engage stakeholders, weaving a web of initiatives that are as compelling as they are effective, ensuring your vision is irresistible and inevitable.

## OCTOBER 25TH

# DYNAMO OF DECEPTION

*"Generate currents of deception with the energy of a dynamo, channeling misinformation to confuse adversaries and clear your path to dominance."*

Embrace the role of a dynamo of deception, where your ability to generate and sustain streams of misinformation can disorient and destabilize opponents. This tactic is particularly effective in environments rife with competition and rivalry, where the ability to obscure true intentions gives you a strategic edge. Use deception as a dynamic force, creating a fog of war that shields your movements and intentions from prying eyes.

Master this strategy by maintaining a constant flow of actions and information that keeps adversaries off-balance. Adjust the intensity and direction of your deceptive currents to suit the situation, ensuring that you always have the upper hand. By controlling the narrative and the flow of information, you pave the way for unimpeded progress toward your goals, securing your position as a formidable player in the game of power.

## OCTOBER 26TH

# ALCHEMIST OF AGENDAS

*"Transform everyday interactions into opportunities, like an alchemist turning base metals into gold, each conversation strategically spun to advance your agenda."*

Embody the role of an alchemist in your daily interactions, where you expertly convert mundane exchanges into strategic victories. This approach requires a keen sense of timing and perception, enabling you to identify and capitalize on opportunities that others might overlook. Use your conversational alchemy to subtly steer discussions in ways that align with your objectives, blending persuasion with insight to mold opinions and decisions.

To excel in this role, practice active listening and thoughtful engagement, ensuring that every interaction is an opportunity to influence and gather information. By treating each conversation as a potential goldmine, you harness the power of dialogue to craft outcomes that significantly benefit your strategic pursuits.

## OCTOBER 27TH

# CHESSMASTER OF CHANGE

*"Anticipate and initiate changes with the foresight of a chessmaster, strategically positioning your pieces to benefit from every shift on the board."*

Approach the ever-changing dynamics of your environment with the analytical eye of a chessmaster. This involves not just reacting to changes but actively shaping them to serve your ends. By anticipating shifts in the landscape, whether in business, politics, or social settings, you position yourself to capitalize on these evolutions before they fully manifest.

Develop a strategic mindset that allows you to see several moves ahead, understanding how different scenarios might unfold and preparing to make the most of them. Align your resources and allies in such a way that no matter how the board changes, you remain in a position of strength, ready to turn any change into an advantage.

## OCTOBER 28TH

# ILLUSIONIST OF INFLUENCE

*"Craft illusions of influence with the skill of an illusionist, making others believe in the power they perceive you to wield."*

Step into the role of an illusionist who masterfully creates perceptions of influence and power. In many arenas, the perception of influence can be as impactful as actual power. By crafting a façade of authority and capability, you can lead others to act in ways that inherently bolster your real position.

Utilize tactics of visibility and mystique to enhance your perceived influence. This might involve strategic public appearances, calculated displays of connection and clout, or controlled leaks of your supposed insider knowledge. The key is to maintain the illusion with consistency and subtlety, ensuring that others see exactly what you want them to see, thus magnifying your actual power through the art of perception.

## OCTOBER 29TH

# GAMBLER OF GAITS

*"Navigate life's uncertainties with the calculated risks of a gambler, knowing when to hold your cards close and when to play them with a flourish."*

Embrace the uncertainties of your professional and personal life with the calculated daring of a seasoned gambler. Understand that not all risks are to be avoided; some are to be embraced, especially when the odds are in your favor. Assess situations with a critical eye, deciding when it's prudent to conceal your strategies and when it's advantageous to lay them out with confidence.

Sharpen your risk assessment skills to make well-informed decisions that balance potential benefits against possible losses. Know that the greatest achievements often come from taking chances, but only those that are carefully considered and strategically timed to maximize impact and reward.

## OCTOBER 30TH

# INVENTOR OF IDEALS

*"Engineer ideals and values with the creativity of an inventor, shaping the principles that guide others to unknowingly follow your lead."*

Position yourself as an inventor in the realm of ideas and values, crafting principles that resonate widely and guide collective behavior. By shaping the foundational ideals of your community or organization, you subtly steer the actions and decisions of others, aligning them with your strategic goals without their explicit awareness.

Focus on creating compelling, forward-thinking ideals that attract support and enthusiasm. This involves understanding the hopes and fears of your audience, crafting messages that speak directly to their desires and concerns. As you embed these invented ideals into the culture around you, you gain the ability to guide large groups subtly but effectively, leveraging shared values to achieve your broader objectives.

## OCTOBER 31ST

# MASTER OF MASQUERADES

*"Orchestrate a masquerade where each disguise is more than mere concealment, serving as a strategic tool in the grand design of your ambitions."*

Master the art of the masquerade, where disguises and deceptions play crucial roles in your strategic playbook. In this complex dance of appearances, each mask you and others wear serves a purpose beyond simple concealment—it's a carefully chosen armor that protects and projects the necessary image to influence and maneuver within your chosen fields.

Become adept at both wearing masks and deciphering those worn by others. Use this knowledge to manipulate social and professional interactions to your advantage. Each masquerade you orchestrate should advance your plans discreetly, allowing you to navigate through layers of social intrigue while keeping your ultimate objectives hidden and your strategies secure.

# NOVEMBER

## NOVEMBER 1ST

# SCULPTOR OF SITUATIONS

*"Mold situations to your advantage with the finesse of a sculptor, shaping each detail to fit your grand design."*

View each situation as a block of marble, ready to be shaped by your strategic hand. As a sculptor of situations, use your creativity and foresight to carve out opportunities and smooth over obstacles. This involves understanding the raw material of your circumstances and seeing the potential within it to create something that aligns perfectly with your objectives.

Approach each challenge with the patience and precision of a master sculptor, carefully removing what doesn't serve your purpose and refining what does. By skillfully shaping situations to fit your grand design, you can turn even the most unpromising scenarios into masterpieces of strategic advantage.

**NOVEMBER 2ND**

# GUARDIAN OF GAMBITS

*"Guard your strategic moves like a fortress, ensuring each gambit is protected and poised for maximum impact."*

Take on the role of a guardian for your strategic gambits, treating each move as a valuable asset that must be shielded from prying eyes and potential sabotage. This requires a balance of vigilance and cunning, as you work to protect your plans while also positioning them for optimal execution.

Develop a robust defense mechanism around your strategies, using secrecy, misdirection, and carefully chosen allies to keep your true intentions hidden. By guarding your gambits effectively, you ensure that when the time comes to act, your moves are both unexpected and unstoppable, securing your path to success.

## NOVEMBER 3RD

# CURATOR OF CONNECTIONS

*"Curate your network with the discernment of a collector, each relationship chosen for its strategic value and potential."*

See yourself as a curator, carefully selecting and nurturing relationships that enhance your influence and advance your goals. Like a collector who chooses each piece for its unique value and contribution to the collection, build a network that supports and amplifies your strategic vision.

Focus on creating meaningful connections with individuals who bring diverse strengths and perspectives to your endeavors. Invest time in maintaining and deepening these relationships, ensuring they remain strong and mutually beneficial. By curating your connections with care, you create a powerful web of influence that can be leveraged to achieve your objectives.

## NOVEMBER 4TH

# WARDEN OF WHISPERS

*"Guard the flow of information with the vigilance of a warden, using whispers to control narratives and influence outcomes."*

Embrace the role of a warden in your professional and personal life, controlling the flow of information with precision and purpose. By managing what is shared and what is kept secret, you can influence narratives and guide the actions of those around you.

Be vigilant about the information that passes through your network, using whispers strategically to plant ideas, shift perceptions, and build alliances. This control over communication allows you to shape the broader narrative to align with your strategic goals, ensuring that your influence remains strong and pervasive.

## NOVEMBER 5TH

# MAESTRO OF MOVEMENTS

*"Conduct your strategic initiatives like a symphony, where each movement is orchestrated for maximum impact and harmony."*

Take the helm as a maestro, conducting your strategic initiatives with the precision and artistry of a symphony. Each movement in your plan should be carefully timed and executed, ensuring that all elements work together harmoniously to create a powerful and cohesive performance.

Approach your initiatives with a clear vision and a detailed plan, adjusting the tempo and intensity as needed to maintain momentum and achieve your goals. By conducting your strategies like a maestro, you ensure that each action contributes to a larger, more impactful outcome, driving your success with the elegance and power of a well-composed symphony.

## NOVEMBER 6TH

# ALCHEMIST OF ALLIANCES

*"Forge alliances with the transformative power of an alchemist, turning base relationships into golden opportunities."*

View your alliances as elements to be transformed through the alchemy of strategic partnership. By carefully selecting and nurturing these relationships, you can turn base connections into valuable assets that significantly advance your goals.

Focus on identifying potential allies whose strengths complement your own and whose objectives align with yours. Invest time and effort in building trust and mutual benefit, creating alliances that are not only strong but also flexible enough to adapt to changing circumstances. Through this alchemical process, you can create powerful partnerships that enhance your influence and drive success.

## NOVEMBER 7TH

# ARCHITECT OF ADVANTAGE

*"Design every move with the foresight of an architect,
building structures of advantage that stand the test of time."*

Think of yourself as an architect of advantage, meticulously designing each move to construct a solid foundation for your success. This involves careful planning and strategic foresight, ensuring that every action you take contributes to a larger, more robust structure of influence and power.

Approach your strategy with a clear blueprint in mind, identifying key opportunities and potential challenges. Build your plans step by step, reinforcing your position with each move. By thinking and acting like an architect, you create a durable and resilient framework that supports your long-term ambitions and withstands the pressures of competition.

## NOVEMBER 8TH

# KEEPER OF KEYS

*"Hold the keys to crucial opportunities, unlocking doors with precision and timing to reveal new pathways to success."*

Holding the keys to hidden opportunities gives you unique power. This role requires discernment and strategic timing to use your keys for maximum impact.

Develop a keen sense of when to reveal your capabilities and when to hold back, ensuring that each key you use opens a pathway that aligns with your broader objectives. By carefully managing these opportunities, you maintain control over your progress and keep competitors guessing, always a step behind.

# MANIPULATOR OF MOMENTS

*"Seize and shape moments with the dexterity of a master manipulator, turning fleeting opportunities into lasting advantages."*

Become a master manipulator of moments, skillfully seizing and shaping opportunities as they arise. This requires not only agility and impeccable timing but also a sharp awareness of your surroundings and an acute understanding of human nature. By honing your ability to read situations and people, you can turn even the briefest chances into significant gains. Recognize the potential in every moment, and be prepared to act with precision and confidence.

Stay attuned to the ebb and flow of events around you, ready to act swiftly and decisively when the right moment presents itself. Use your abilities to influence outcomes, ensuring each moment you manipulate contributes to your strategic goals. By mastering this approach, you can transform fleeting opportunities into lasting advantages, consistently advancing your position.

## NOVEMBER 10TH

# ENCHANTER OF ENDEAVORS

*"Enchant your endeavors with a touch of magic, making each initiative irresistible and compelling to those who encounter it."*

Infuse your initiatives with the charm and allure of a master enchanter, making them not only effective but also irresistibly captivating. Present your schemes and projects in a way that highlights their benefits and manipulates the emotions and interests of your audience.

Craft compelling narratives and presentations that draw people in, making them eager to support your ambitions. By enchanting your initiatives with persuasive storytelling and strategic appeal, you ensure they stand out and command the attention and resources needed to succeed, turning your vision into reality with an irresistible allure.

## NOVEMBER 11TH

# MASTERMIND OF MOMENTUM

*"Build and sustain momentum like a mastermind, ensuring each step forward accelerates your progress towards ultimate success."*

Take on the role of a mastermind, ruthlessly maintaining and amplifying momentum in your projects and initiatives. Recognize that sustained effort and continuous progress are key to achieving your long-term ambitions. By meticulously planning and executing each step, you create a relentless flow of energy that propels you forward.

Develop strategies to keep the momentum unyielding, even when confronting obstacles. Celebrate small victories as fuel for your drive, stay adaptable, and keep your vision sharp and compelling. By acting as a mastermind of momentum, you ensure that each action builds on the last, creating an unstoppable force driving you toward your ultimate objectives.

# NOVEMBER 12TH

## GUARDIAN OF GOALS

*"Protect and prioritize your goals with the vigilance of a guardian, ensuring that every action you take aligns with your ultimate ambitions."*

Assume the role of a vigilant guardian, ruthlessly protecting your goals and ensuring that every decision and action aligns with your long-term ambitions. This requires constant awareness and unwavering dedication, as well as the ability to prioritize tasks and resources with precision.

Stay focused on your objectives, eliminating distractions and neutralizing potential threats that could derail your progress. By maintaining this level of vigilance, you ensure that each step you take fortifies your path to dominance, safeguarding your rise to power and success.

## NOVEMBER 13TH

# WEAVER OF WONDERS

*"Create extraordinary outcomes by weaving together diverse elements, transforming the ordinary into something truly wonderful."*

Embrace the role of a master weaver, skillfully combining disparate elements to create extraordinary outcomes. Recognize the potential in various resources, ideas, and relationships, and manipulate them to enhance their individual value for your grand design.

Develop your ability to see connections and possibilities where others see none, using cunning and innovation to transform the mundane into something formidable. By weaving these elements together, you craft a tapestry of success that commands attention and awe, showcasing your power to turn potential into dominance.

## NOVEMBER 14TH

# SEER OF SUCCESS

*"Envision your success with the clarity of a seer, allowing your foresight to guide your actions and decisions."*

Adopt the perspective of a seer, using your foresight to envision your path to dominance clearly. Set a ruthless vision for your future and use that vision to dictate your actions and decisions. By keeping your ambitions in sight, you can navigate challenges and seize opportunities with confidence and purpose.

Hone your ability to predict potential outcomes and plan accordingly, ensuring each step aligns with your vision of supremacy. By acting as a seer of success, you maintain a focused and proactive approach, allowing your foresight to drive your relentless progress toward ultimate power.

## NOVEMBER 15TH

# STRATEGIST OF SERENITY

*"Maintain calm and control in all situations, using serenity as a strategic tool to navigate challenges and opportunities."*

Take on the role of a ruthless strategist, wielding calm and composure as weapons to navigate challenges and seize opportunities. In high-pressure situations, maintaining your calm allows you to think clearly and make calculated decisions, turning potential chaos into strategic advantage.

Master techniques to stay grounded and focused, regardless of external turmoil. Use your serenity to manipulate those around you, fostering an environment of control and confidence. By mastering this approach, you turn serenity into a formidable strategic asset, ensuring you remain in command and effective, even in the most challenging situations.

## NOVEMBER 16TH

# DESIGNER OF DESTINIES

*"Shape your future with the intent and precision of a designer, crafting each step to align with your ultimate destiny."*

Approach your life and career as a master designer shapes a masterpiece, with intent and precision in every step. Set ruthless goals and meticulously plan each move to align with your ultimate vision of power. By taking a calculated and strategic approach, you forge a pathway that leads directly to your inevitable dominance.

Design your actions and decisions to build towards your long-term ambitions. Consider the impact of each choice and how it serves your grand design. By acting as a designer of destinies, you craft a cohesive and strategic plan that ensures your rise to supremacy and control.

## NOVEMBER 17TH

# CATALYST OF CHANGE

*"Act as a catalyst for change, initiating and driving transformations that lead to growth and progress."*

Embrace the role of a catalyst, igniting change and driving transformations that lead to your rise in power. This requires a proactive mindset and the audacity to take risks, challenging the status quo to create superior opportunities and outcomes.

Identify areas where change is needed and seize the initiative to drive that change. Use your influence and resources to manipulate and inspire others, building unstoppable momentum toward your ambitions. By acting as a catalyst of change, you ensure relentless progress, creating a dynamic environment that fosters innovation and domination.

## NOVEMBER 18TH

# ENGINEER OF ENVIRONMENTS

*"Construct environments that foster success, using your skills to shape the conditions in which you and others thrive."*

Take on the role of an engineer, meticulously designing and constructing environments that support your path to power. This involves creating conditions that encourage productivity, creativity, and collaboration, ensuring that you and your minions thrive.

Focus on building physical, social, and organizational environments that align with your grand ambitions. Use your cunning to identify what works and what doesn't, making ruthless adjustments to optimize conditions. By acting as an engineer of environments, you lay the foundation for sustained dominance and growth.

## NOVEMBER 19TH

# SCULPTOR OF SUCCESS

*"Carve out your path to success with the precision and care of a sculptor, shaping each opportunity to fit your vision."*

Adopt the mindset of a sculptor, carefully shaping your path to success with precision and intent. This involves identifying opportunities and challenges as raw materials, using your skills and vision to carve out a path that aligns with your goals.

Approach each step with attention to detail and a focus on the bigger picture. Make deliberate choices that refine and enhance your journey, ensuring that every move contributes to your overall vision of success. By acting as a sculptor of success, you create a path that is uniquely yours, shaped by your hands and guided by your ambition.

## NOVEMBER 20TH

# VISIONARY OF VICTORY

*"Lead with the foresight of a visionary, inspiring others and guiding your team to achieve shared victories."*

Embrace the role of a visionary overlord, using your foresight and cunning to lead others toward shared conquests. Craft a clear and compelling vision that commands and unites your minions, guiding them with unshakable confidence.

Cultivate your ability to see the grand design and anticipate future shifts, using this insight to make strategic decisions that inspire and manipulate those around you. By acting as a visionary of victory, you create a sense of purpose and direction that drives your team to achieve greatness, ensuring collective dominance and fulfillment.

## NOVEMBER 21ST

# GUARDIAN OF RUTHLESS GROWTH

*"Relentlessly pursue your development and that of your allies, ensuring continuous improvement and dominance."*

Embrace your inner villain by adopting the role of a guardian of ruthless growth, both for yourself and those aligned with you. Cultivate an environment where relentless improvement is not just encouraged but demanded. By driving continuous progress, you pave the way for long-term dominance and success.

Focus on providing resources and opportunities for learning and advancement, but do so strategically. Identify and support only those who demonstrate loyalty and potential. By acting as a guardian of ruthless growth, you create a culture of excellence that benefits you and your closest allies, driving collective achievement and personal gain.

## NOVEMBER 22ND

# STRATEGIST OF SINISTER SYNERGY

*"Forge powerful alliances and partnerships, leveraging synergy to amplify your influence and achieve mutual goals."*

Channel your inner villain by becoming a strategist of sinister synergy, where your primary objective is to create and exploit partnerships that enhance your power. Identify potential allies who can amplify your strengths and work collaboratively to achieve common, yet self-serving, objectives.

Develop your ability to build trust selectively and create win-win scenarios that ultimately benefit you the most. By mastering the art of sinister synergy, you multiply the impact of your efforts through collective action, ensuring that your goals are met and your influence is expanded.

## NOVEMBER 23RD

# CATALYST OF CALCULATED CHAOS

*"Spark innovation and disruption with strategic mischief,
turning bold ideas into actionable schemes."*

Embrace the chaos by becoming a catalyst of calculated disruption, igniting change within yourself and your circle. Encourage bold, out-of-the-box thinking, but always with a strategic twist. Transform innovative concepts into actionable plans that serve your ends and shake up the status quo.

Foster a culture where experimentation is valued and failures are seen as opportunities for growth. Encourage creative mischief that aligns with your goals. By acting as a catalyst of calculated chaos, you keep your environment dynamic and adaptable, always ready to seize new opportunities and outmaneuver your rivals.

# ARCHITECT OF AUTONOMOUS CONTROL

*"Design systems and structures that empower selective autonomy, enabling trusted individuals to excel while maintaining overarching control."*

Act as an architect of autonomous control, creating environments that empower select individuals to take ownership of their roles while ensuring you retain ultimate control. This involves designing systems and structures that encourage self-reliance and accountability, but only for those who have proven their loyalty and competence.

Provide the tools and support necessary for autonomy, but maintain clear goals and oversight. By fostering a culture of controlled independence, you ensure that your trusted allies can thrive and contribute effectively, while you remain the ultimate authority.

## NOVEMBER 25TH

# DIPLOMAT OF DECEPTION

*"Navigate complex interactions with the finesse of a diplomat, using strategic deceit to build bridges and manipulate outcomes."*

Adopt the role of a diplomat of deception, skillfully managing interactions with a blend of tact and strategic deceit. This involves understanding different perspectives and using subtle manipulation to find common ground, build alliances, and resolve conflicts in ways that serve your interests.

Cultivate the ability to listen actively and communicate convincingly, employing deception where necessary to achieve your goals. Use diplomacy to turn potential adversaries into pawns and allies. By mastering this approach, you strengthen your position and create a network of influence that enhances your power.

## NOVEMBER 26TH

# CHAMPION OF RUTHLESS CHANGE

*"Lead transformations with an iron will, guiding your team through upheavals to achieve unparalleled success."*

Embrace the role of a champion of ruthless change, leading transformations with determination and an uncompromising approach. Guide your team through periods of upheaval, ensuring they are motivated and driven to embrace new directions that align with your grand vision.

Communicate the necessity and benefits of change with conviction. Provide the resources and support needed to navigate transitions, but expect results. By acting as a champion of ruthless change, you inspire others to adapt and excel, driving collective progress and securing your dominance.

## NOVEMBER 27TH

# CONDUCTOR OF CONTROLLED CONFIDENCE

*"Instill unwavering confidence in yourself and others,
leading with poise and calculated assurance."*

Take on the role of a conductor of controlled confidence, leading with poise and calculated assurance. In high-pressure situations, maintain a calm and confident demeanor, inspiring trust and belief in your vision. Use this controlled confidence to manipulate perceptions and maintain control.

Build your self-confidence through preparation and strategic planning. Encourage and support others in developing their confidence, but always in ways that align with your objectives. By acting as a conductor of controlled confidence, you create a powerful and influential presence that drives success.

## NOVEMBER 28TH

# VISIONARY OF VEXATION

*"Create and communicate disruptive value, ensuring that every action and decision challenges the status quo and advances your agenda."*

Adopt the perspective of a visionary of vexation, consistently creating and communicating value that disrupts the norm. Understand and articulate your disruptive principles, ensuring that every action and decision aligns with these values to further your agenda.

Build a clear and compelling vision that highlights the transformative impact you aim to achieve. Communicate this vision effectively, ensuring that others understand and support your commitment to challenging the status quo. By acting as a visionary of vexation, you build a strong foundation of influence and drive long-term success.

## NOVEMBER 29TH

# STEWARD OF STRATEGIC SUBTERFUGE

*"Guide strategic initiatives with the care of a steward, using subterfuge to align actions with long-term goals."*

Assume the role of a steward of strategic subterfuge, guiding initiatives with careful consideration and strategic deception. Take a thoughtful approach to planning and execution, ensuring that each step contributes to your broader vision while concealing your true intentions.

Anticipate challenges and opportunities, adjusting your strategies as needed. Balance short-term actions with long-term objectives, using subterfuge to protect your plans and maintain control. By acting as a steward of strategic subterfuge, you create a legacy of thoughtful and effective leadership.

## NOVEMBER 30TH

# PIONEER OF PERNICIOUS POSSIBILITIES

*"Explore new frontiers with the curiosity and cunning of a pioneer, discovering opportunities and forging paths to power."*

Embrace the role of a pioneer of pernicious possibilities, exploring new frontiers with curiosity and cunning. Seek out opportunities that others might overlook, taking bold steps to forge paths to power. Push beyond the boundaries of what is known and comfortable, using your strategic mind to discover and exploit new possibilities.

Cultivate a mindset of exploration and innovation, always looking for ways to expand your influence and challenge the status quo. Encourage others to join you in this journey, fostering a culture of continuous growth and strategic advantage. By acting as a pioneer of pernicious possibilities, you lead the way to new achievements and secure your position of power.

# December

## DECEMBER 1ST

# MANIPULATOR OF MINDSETS

*"Shift perspectives with the finesse of a manipulator, molding mindsets to align with your strategic objectives."*

Step into the role of a manipulator of mindsets, skillfully influencing how others think and perceive situations. Use psychological tactics and strategic communication to reshape opinions and beliefs, aligning them with your overarching goals. By controlling the narrative, you can guide decisions and actions in your favor.

Develop your skills in persuasive communication and emotional intelligence. Understand what motivates others and use this knowledge to craft messages that resonate deeply, leading them to adopt the perspectives you promote. By mastering this approach, you ensure that your influence extends beyond actions to the very thoughts and attitudes of those around you.

# COMMANDER OF CHARADES

*"Direct the grand charade of life with the authority of a commander, using deception and misdirection to maintain control."*

Take on the role of a commander of charades, where life is a grand performance and you are the director. Use deception and misdirection as your tools to control the narrative and keep your true intentions hidden. Ensure that each action and statement is part of a carefully constructed facade that serves your strategic aims.

Focus on crafting believable and compelling charades that keep others engaged and misled. Maintain a firm grasp on the story you are presenting, adjusting it as necessary to keep your audience guessing. By commanding the charade, you maintain control over perceptions and outcomes, steering events to your advantage.

## DECEMBER 3RD

# SCULPTOR OF SHADOWS

*"Shape the unseen elements of your strategy with the precision of a sculptor, crafting shadows that conceal and reveal as needed."*

Embrace the role of a sculptor of shadows, where you meticulously shape the unseen aspects of your strategy. Use the shadows to conceal your true intentions and reveal only what is necessary to guide others' perceptions and actions. This approach allows you to operate with a level of secrecy and subtlety that enhances your strategic advantage.

Develop your ability to manage information and visibility, ensuring that you control what is seen and what remains hidden. Use this control to manipulate outcomes and protect your interests. By mastering the art of sculpting shadows, you create a dynamic and adaptable strategy that keeps you one step ahead of your rivals.

## DECEMBER 4TH

# ENCHANTER OF EVASION

*"Master the art of evasion with the skill of an enchanter, escaping scrutiny while advancing your hidden agendas."*

Adopt the persona of an enchanter of evasion, where your primary skill is avoiding detection and scrutiny while pursuing your hidden agendas. Use charm, distraction, and misdirection to keep others focused elsewhere, allowing you to maneuver freely and execute your plans without interference.

Hone your skills in evasion by practicing subtlety and discretion in all your actions. Create plausible diversions and maintain a low profile when necessary, ensuring that your true objectives remain concealed. By mastering evasion, you protect your strategies and maintain the element of surprise.

## DECEMBER 5TH

# SAGE OF SUBVERSION

*"Subvert expectations with the wisdom of a sage, turning conventional wisdom on its head to achieve your aims."*

Embrace your inner villain by becoming a sage of subversion, where your wisdom allows you to upend conventional thinking and create new pathways to success. Use your knowledge and insight to challenge established norms and introduce innovative ideas that serve your goals.

Cultivate an understanding of the systems and structures you wish to subvert, identifying weaknesses and opportunities for disruption. Employ strategic thinking to introduce subversive tactics that appear beneficial or innocuous but ultimately advance your hidden agendas. By mastering subversion, you can reshape the landscape to your advantage.

## DECEMBER 6TH

# ALCHEMIST OF AMBIGUITY

*"Transform clarity into ambiguity with the deftness of an alchemist, creating confusion that obscures your true motives."*

Assume the role of an alchemist of ambiguity, where your skill lies in turning clear situations into ambiguous ones that obscure your true intentions. Use this ambiguity to your advantage, creating confusion that prevents others from understanding your motives and plans.

Develop your ability to introduce complexity and uncertainty into situations, making it difficult for others to predict your actions or uncover your strategies. By fostering ambiguity, you protect your interests and maintain control over the narrative, ensuring that you can maneuver without opposition.

## DECEMBER 7TH

# TACTICIAN OF TENSION

*"Create and manage tension with the precision of a tactician, using it to drive decisions and actions in your favor."*

Step into the role of a tactician of tension, where you skillfully create and manage tension to influence decisions and actions. Use this tension to keep others on edge and more likely to make choices that benefit you. By controlling the levels of tension, you can guide the behavior of those around you.

Focus on understanding the dynamics of tension and how it affects people. Use this knowledge to introduce or alleviate pressure strategically, ensuring that it always serves your purposes. By mastering the art of tension, you maintain a powerful tool for manipulation and control.

## DECEMBER 8TH

# ORACLE OF OPPORTUNISM

*"Seize opportunities with the foresight of an oracle, turning every situation to your advantage."*

Embrace the role of an oracle of opportunism, where you possess the foresight to identify and exploit opportunities as they arise. Use your keen sense of timing and situational awareness to turn every event into a chance to advance your goals.

Develop your ability to quickly assess situations and recognize potential benefits. Act decisively and strategically to capitalize on these opportunities, ensuring that you are always positioned to gain from them. By mastering opportunism, you ensure that you can adapt and thrive in any environment.

## DECEMBER 9TH

# MANIPULATOR OF MYSTERIES

*"Craft and control mysteries with the finesse of a master manipulator, keeping others intrigued and off-balance."*

Adopt the role of a manipulator of mysteries, where you create and control enigmatic scenarios that keep others intrigued and uncertain. Use these mysteries to divert attention, create interest, and keep your true intentions hidden.

Focus on developing your ability to weave complex and captivating narratives that draw people in while concealing your true objectives. Use ambiguity and misdirection to maintain control over the situation, ensuring that others remain off-balance and unable to predict your next move. By mastering mysteries, you create a powerful tool for influence and control.

## DECEMBER 10TH

# THE COLDNESS OF CALLOUSNESS

*"Callousness is the armor that shields against empathy, turning emotional detachment into strategic advantage."*

Adopt callousness as your shield, recognizing that emotional detachment provides clarity and focus in decision-making. Like a military commander making tough strategic choices, use your lack of empathy to navigate challenges effectively.

Approach each situation pragmatically, prioritizing your goals over sentiments. Callousness, when balanced with strategic thinking, offers the clarity needed to achieve your most ambitious objectives. It allows you to focus on the bigger picture and make decisions others might avoid.

Mastering callousness lets you navigate complex scenarios with precision, ensuring your path to success remains unclouded by emotional distractions.

## DECEMBER 11TH

# PROVOCATEUR OF POWER

*"Stir emotions and provoke reactions with the subtlety of a provocateur, using them to consolidate and expand your influence."*

Embrace the role of a provocateur of power, where your actions and words are designed to elicit strong emotions and provoke reactions. Use this ability to manipulate the emotional landscape, guiding people's responses to serve your strategic goals. By stirring emotions, you can rally support, create divisions among your adversaries, and strengthen your position.

Focus on understanding the emotional triggers of those around you, using this knowledge to craft messages and actions that provoke the desired responses. By mastering this approach, you can turn emotional dynamics into a powerful tool for consolidating and expanding your influence.

## DECEMBER 12TH

# ENGINEER OF ENIGMA

*"Construct puzzles and riddles with the precision of an engineer, using them to obscure your true intentions and plans."*

Assume the role of an engineer of enigma, where you design complex puzzles and riddles that mask your true intentions and strategies. Use these enigmas to keep your adversaries guessing, ensuring they expend their energy trying to decipher your plans rather than countering them.

Develop your ability to create multi-layered scenarios that are difficult to unravel. Use these constructs to lead others down false paths or to keep them occupied while you maneuver behind the scenes. By mastering the art of the enigma, you protect your strategies and maintain the element of surprise.

## DECEMBER 13TH

# DIRECTOR OF DECEPTION

*"Direct the flow of information and misinformation with the expertise of a director, crafting a narrative that serves your purposes."*

Step into the role of a director of deception, where you control both the information and misinformation that shapes the perceptions of others. Craft a narrative that aligns with your strategic goals, ensuring that those around you see only what you want them to see.

Focus on managing the flow of information carefully, deciding what to reveal and what to conceal. Use misinformation to mislead and create advantageous situations. By mastering this approach, you control the narrative and steer events to your favor.

## DECEMBER 14TH

# MASTER OF MASKS

*"Don various masks with the versatility of a master actor, using each persona to manipulate and influence your audience."*

Embrace your inner villain by becoming a master of masks, adept at adopting various personas to suit different situations and objectives. Each mask allows you to interact with your audience in ways that manipulate and influence their perceptions and actions.

Develop your ability to switch seamlessly between different roles, each crafted to achieve specific outcomes. Whether you need to be charming, authoritative, or enigmatic, ensure that your chosen mask enhances your strategic position. By mastering this approach, you can navigate diverse scenarios with ease and effectiveness.

## DECEMBER 15TH

# ARCHITECT OF AMBUSH

*"Plan and execute strategic ambushes with the precision of
an architect, ensuring that your moves are both unexpected
and devastating."*

Adopt the role of an architect of ambush, where you design and implement surprise attacks that catch your adversaries off guard. Use this tactic to create opportunities that are both unexpected and highly advantageous, ensuring your moves have maximum impact.

Focus on meticulous planning and timing, ensuring that your ambushes are well-coordinated and effective. Use deception and misdirection to set the stage, leading your targets into traps from which they cannot escape. By mastering the art of the ambush, you can dominate your strategic landscape and eliminate threats with precision.

# BARON OF BETRAYAL

*"Leverage betrayal as a strategic tool, using it to dismantle alliances and consolidate your power."*

Embrace the role of a baron of betrayal, where you use treachery as a calculated strategy to weaken your adversaries and strengthen your position. Understand that betrayal, when timed correctly, can dismantle alliances and create chaos that you can exploit.

Develop your ability to identify and exploit vulnerabilities within alliances. Use charm and manipulation to gain trust before executing your betrayal at the most opportune moment. By mastering this approach, you ensure that your enemies are left isolated and vulnerable, while you emerge stronger.

## DECEMBER 17TH

# SENTINEL OF SECRETS

*"Guard your secrets with the vigilance of a sentinel, using them as weapons in your strategic arsenal."*

Assume the role of a sentinel of secrets, where you protect your most valuable information with utmost care. Understand that secrets can be powerful weapons, providing you with leverage over others and shielding your true intentions.

Focus on developing robust methods for safeguarding your secrets, ensuring that only those you trust implicitly have access. Use your knowledge strategically, revealing information only when it serves your purposes. By mastering this approach, you maintain a position of strength and control.

## DECEMBER 18TH

# STRATEGIST OF SILENCE

*"Utilize silence as a strategic tool, allowing it to create unease and drive others to reveal their intentions."*

Embrace the role of a strategist of silence, understanding that what you don't say can be as powerful as what you do. Use silence strategically to create unease, encouraging others to fill the void with information that can reveal their intentions and weaknesses.

Develop your ability to remain silent at critical moments, using this tactic to gain psychological advantage. By mastering silence, you create opportunities to gather intelligence and manipulate conversations without revealing your own plans.

## DECEMBER 19TH

# MANIPULATOR OF MEMORIES

*"Influence perceptions of the past with the subtlety of a manipulator, reshaping memories to serve your narrative."*

Take on the role of a manipulator of memories, where you subtly influence how others remember past events. Use this power to reshape perceptions and create a narrative that aligns with your strategic goals.

Focus on planting suggestions and guiding conversations in ways that alter recollections. By reshaping memories, you can control how the past is perceived, influencing current attitudes and future decisions in your favor.

## DECEMBER 20TH

# OVERLORD OF ENMITY

*"Foster and exploit rivalries with the authority of an overlord, using enmity to weaken your enemies and strengthen your rule."*

Embrace your inner villain by becoming an overlord of enmity, where you cultivate and exploit rivalries to your advantage. Use these conflicts to distract and weaken your adversaries, ensuring that their energies are spent fighting each other rather than opposing you.

Develop your ability to identify potential rivalries and fan the flames of discord. Use manipulation and deceit to intensify conflicts, positioning yourself as the neutral party who can benefit from their mutual destruction. By mastering this approach, you solidify your dominance and ensure that your enemies remain divided and powerless.

## DECEMBER 21ST

# BROKER OF BETRAYALS

*"Broker betrayals with the skill of a mercenary, turning loyalty into a commodity that you can trade for power."*

Step into the role of a broker of betrayals, where loyalty is a flexible commodity you can manipulate. Encourage alliances that are built on shaky grounds, knowing you can exploit these relationships to your advantage when the time is right. Use betrayal as a currency, trading it to consolidate your power and eliminate potential threats.

Develop your ability to read people and situations, identifying when and where betrayals can be most effectively orchestrated. By mastering the art of betrayal, you create a dynamic environment where your control is maintained through calculated disloyalty and strategic deception.

## DECEMBER 22ND

# MASTER OF MANIPULATIONS

*"Orchestrate manipulations with the grace of a master, ensuring that every move you make is part of a grander design. "*

Adopt the role of a master of manipulation, where every action and decision is part of a meticulously crafted plan. Use your skills to subtly influence those around you, ensuring that they act in ways that serve your greater purpose. By orchestrating these manipulations, you maintain a tight grip on your environment, guiding events to align with your ambitions.

Focus on understanding the motivations and weaknesses of others, using this knowledge to direct their actions without them realizing it. By mastering manipulation, you control the narrative and shape the future to your advantage.

## DECEMBER 23RD

# ARCHITECT OF ANARCHY

*"Design chaos with the precision of an architect, using it to disrupt your enemies and clear your path to power."*

Embrace the chaos by becoming an architect of anarchy, where you strategically create disorder to dismantle the structures of your adversaries. Use this chaos to weaken their foundations and clear obstacles from your path, ensuring that you emerge as the dominant force.

Develop your ability to introduce and manage chaos, ensuring that it serves your strategic objectives. By mastering the creation of anarchy, you turn disruption into a powerful tool that paves the way for your ascendancy.

## DECEMBER 24TH

# SCULPTOR OF SCHEMES

*"Craft intricate schemes with the finesse of a sculptor, ensuring that every detail serves your grand strategy."*

Take on the role of a sculptor of schemes, where each plan you devise is a work of art, meticulously crafted to advance your goals. Use your creativity and strategic mind to design plots that are both complex and effective, ensuring that every detail aligns with your larger vision.

Focus on the precision of your schemes, anticipating potential pitfalls and preparing contingencies. By mastering the art of scheming, you create a web of influence and control that is both robust and flexible, capable of adapting to any challenge.

## DECEMBER 25TH

# WARDEN OF WILES

*"Guard your cunning strategies with the vigilance of a warden, using wiles to outsmart and outmaneuver your opponents."*

Embrace your inner villain by becoming a warden of wiles, where your cunning strategies are protected and utilized with utmost care. Use your wiles to outsmart and outmaneuver those who stand in your way, ensuring that you always have the upper hand.

Develop your ability to think several steps ahead, using deceit and cleverness to navigate complex situations. By mastering the use of wiles, you maintain control over your plans and consistently outpace your rivals.

## DECEMBER 26TH

# SORCERER OF SECRETS

*"Guard and wield secrets with the power of a sorcerer, using them to manipulate and control your environment."*

Assume the role of a sorcerer of secrets, where the knowledge you hold is both a shield and a weapon. Use secrets to manipulate those around you, ensuring that you can influence events and outcomes to suit your needs. By guarding these secrets carefully, you maintain an aura of mystery and power.

Focus on acquiring and protecting valuable information, using it strategically to enhance your influence. By mastering the art of secrecy, you control the flow of knowledge and use it to maintain your position of power.

## DECEMBER 27TH

# MASTER OF MACHINATIONS

*"Engineer complex machinations with the skill of a master, ensuring that every scheme strengthens your grip on power."*

Adopt the role of a master of machinations, where you engineer complex schemes that fortify your control. Use your strategic mind to design plots that are intricate and far-reaching, ensuring that every move you make strengthens your position.

Develop your ability to anticipate and counter potential threats, using your machinations to keep adversaries off-balance. By mastering this approach, you create a network of influence and control that is unassailable.

## DECEMBER 28TH

# CONQUEROR OF CHAOS

*"Embrace and harness chaos with the prowess of a conqueror, turning turmoil into a tool for domination."*

Step into the role of a conqueror of chaos, where you not only survive disorder but thrive in it. Use chaos as a tool to dismantle the plans of your enemies and create opportunities for your ascent. By harnessing turmoil, you can dominate any situation and emerge as the clear leader.

Develop your ability to navigate and exploit chaotic environments, ensuring that you can turn any disruption to your advantage. By mastering chaos, you maintain a position of strength and flexibility, always ready to seize control.

## DECEMBER 29TH

# PUPPET MASTER OF POWER

*"Control the strings of power with the deftness of a puppet master, ensuring that every move is orchestrated to maintain your dominance."*

Assume the role of a puppet master of power, where you skillfully control the actions and decisions of those around you. Use your influence to pull the strings, ensuring that every move made by others serves your strategic goals. By orchestrating events from behind the scenes, you maintain an iron grip on your environment.

Focus on developing your network of influence, using manipulation and persuasion to direct the actions of key players. By mastering this approach, you ensure that your control is both subtle and absolute.

## DECEMBER 30TH

# EMPEROR OF ENIGMA

*"Rule with the enigmatic authority of an emperor, using mystery and secrecy to keep your power unchallenged."*

Embrace the role of an emperor of enigma, where your rule is characterized by mystery and secrecy. Use these elements to keep your subjects and rivals in awe, ensuring that they are never quite sure of your next move. By maintaining an enigmatic presence, you prevent challenges to your authority and keep everyone guessing.

Develop your ability to cloak your true intentions in layers of secrecy, creating an aura of invincibility. By mastering the art of enigma, you ensure that your power remains unchallenged and your rule undisputed.

## DECEMBER 31ST

# KING OF CONTROL

*"Reign supreme as the king of control, maintaining your power by keeping everyone in check and manipulating the chessboard of life."*

Assume the ultimate role as the king of control, where your reign is defined by an unyielding grip on power. Use manipulation, influence, and strategic foresight to keep every individual and situation under your control. Ensure that every move on the chessboard of life is orchestrated to reinforce your dominance and suppress any potential threats.

Develop a deep understanding of human nature and organizational dynamics, using this knowledge to maintain a delicate balance of power. By mastering the art of control, you ensure that your kingdom remains secure, your authority unchallenged, and your legacy enduring.

# A Final Note

As you finish this journey through the shadows, we hope these pages have imparted valuable insights and practical wisdom to harness your hidden strengths. Embracing your inner villain isn't about malice; it's about understanding and utilizing every aspect of your character to achieve your fullest potential.

May you continue to explore, grow, and conquer with confidence and cunning. Remember, the shadows are not something to be feared but a powerful part of who you are. Step boldly into your potential, and let your inner strength guide you.

We would love to hear your thoughts on this book. Please scan the barcode below to leave a review.

With gratitude and best wishes for your journey ahead.

www.ingramcontent.com/pod-product-compliance
Lightning Source LLC
Chambersburg PA
CBHW051037250726
48656CB00001B/8